Make it Fun and Get it Done!

MONEY GAMES

Debt Freedom for Couples

*Color your way to Financial Freedom - with these fun
Goal Trackers and Savings Challenges*

Heidi Ifland Nash

Creator of Debt Free Charts

HB
BOOKS

Published by HB Books

debtfreecharts.com

Cover by Heidi Ifland Nash

Illustrations by Heidi Ifland Nash, Jennifer Trafton

ISBN 979-8-9881317-1-7 paperback

Why Should You Use This Book

Wouldn't it be amazing to feel financially secure and confident as a couple? Let's face it, money can be a bit tricky to navigate. Saving is hard, resisting overspending is challenging, and climbing out of financial holes can feel impossible. It's frustrating when there's barely any money left at the end of the month, and the holidays always catch us off guard.

You're not alone in this struggle. Many couples find it tough to establish new money habits and feel overwhelmed by the task. But here's the good news: you're holding a simple solution right here in your hands.

This book is the secret sauce to visual goal tracking. These trackers transform the chore of managing money into an exciting game. By using them together, you'll stay motivated, focused, and right on track.

As you color in your progress toward your financial goals, you'll start seeing money in a whole new light. It's not just about coloring; it's about visualizing your progress and making it tangible.

In Atomic Habits, James Clear explains that you can build a new habit by making it Obvious, Attractive, Easy, and Satisfying. Our charts do exactly that. They make it easy for you to track your progress, keep you engaged with their fun designs, and provide a satisfying sense of achievement with every space you color.

No matter how messy your finances may seem, this fun-filled book has got your back. Say goodbye to financial stress and hello to a more enjoyable and successful financial journey as a couple.

But hey, don't take my word for it. Hear what some of the 200,000+ incredible people who have used these tracking charts have to say:

"Debt Free Charts are just so motivating and perfect! They really do help me stay on track. There's that little thrill as you color things in and see your progress. As I pay something off and get to finish coloring everything in... I just want to frame them! "- Teena Marie

"Just what I needed - Adulting with Debt Free Charts is just another level. I love using these charts to track down my savings and debts. It's so satisfying coloring while making a progress." - Stephanie VV

Strangely addictive - I was terrible with money in the past. These charts make it easier for me to track my savings and goals. They make me want to save more quicker just to colour in more spaces - it's truly odd. I've saved an emergency fund and paid off a credit card using these sheets. If you are a visual person I would highly recommend them." - Kylie Anderson

So if you're ready to take control of your finances and start building a brighter financial future together, it's time to dive into the Money Games - Debt Freedom for Couples book! Let's do this!

How to Use this Book

Most of the Trackers have 100 spaces to fill in (others will be indicated, usually on the bottom tracker). Divide your Goal by the number of spaces on the chart to get the amount each space is worth. Color in the spaces as you pay off debt or save up.

The coloring games and trackers are meant to be a visual motivator, and won't always be to-the-penny accurate.

Also included is an optional account Balance Tracker on the back of most trackers so you can keep track of a more precise balance if you like. Each time you make a payment, make an entry with your new balance.

For debt payoff, be sure you are tracking your balance, and not your payments. The coloring trackers will not take into account the interest paid, just the balance getting smaller. If you would like to keep track of the precise balance you can use the Balance Tracker on the back of the chart.

The light-weight paper was chosen to keep the cost affordable.

Coloring with colored pencils or no-bleed pens like gel pens will give the best result. However, since the charts are not back to back with each other, you could use markers if desired. Do be aware that they could bleed through and show on your balance tracker on the back. Test the bleed of your pens on this last page before diving in.

The first half of this book has charts to help you get out of debt, the remainder are for savings goals.

You may wonder why the book isn't ALL debt payoff charts, and that is because part of getting out of debt is saving up ahead of time for expenses. You must get to the point of having savings for things like Christmas, birthdays, travel, taxes, car repair, and so on. If you aren't saving for these things WHILE paying off debt, you will end up back in the same place when those expenses come up.

What's included:
- 2 Habit Trackers
- 3 Starter Emergency Fund & Emergency Fund Refill
- 15 Debt Payoff Games & Challenges- Credit Card, Car Loan, and lots that aren't labeled.
- 34 Savings Goals & Challenges - Christmas, Birthdays, Travel, etc.

There are dozens of Savings Trackers with lots of variety in this book, and most are unthemed. Use them for timed challenges, amount challenges, sinking funds, and other savings goals. Find the one that gets you excited to save and get started!

Detailed instructions are at the beginning of each section, and basic instructions are on the back of each tracker.

I've designed the pages with wider margins near the book spine so if you want you can cut them out of the book if desired. On the back of each chart is a faint cut line (a craft knife might be helpful with this). Put them on your fridge, slip them into your budget binder or planner, or take them with you to track your progress while out and about.

Be sure to look for our other Money Games books coming soon like:
Family Edition   Homeowners Edition
Savings Edition   Investing Edition   and more!

Months of the Year Lettering - a Year-long challenge

Three ways to use:

- **Habit Tracker** - choose two colors (like red/green) and color in one color the days you did your habit, and the other color the days you did not. Cooking Dinner, Packing Lunch, Tracking your Spending, are all great habits to work on that help your finances!
- **Spending Tracker** - Use a different color for each of the following: No Spend, Planned Spend, Unplanned Spend
- **Mood Tracker** - Like a Year in Pixels, but waaay cuter! Write the moods you want to track along the bottom, color code each mood, then fill in the days with the main mood of the day.

Got More Money Goals?

Look for our other Money Games book editions like:
Investing Edition, Family Edition, Super Savings Edition, and More!

Plus there are dozens of FREE downloadable Debt Payoff Charts and lots of fun printable Savings Goal Charts at debtfreecharts.com

JANUARY FEBRUARY MARCH
APRIL MAY
JUNE JULY
AUGUST SEPTEMBER
OCTOBER
NOVEMBER DECEMBER

Months of the Year Lettering - a Year-long challenge

Three ways to use:

- **Habit Tracker** - choose two colors (like red/green) and color in one color the days you did your habit, and the other color the days you did not. Cooking Dinner, Packing Lunch, Tracking your Spending, are all great habits to work on that help your finances!
- **Spending Tracker** - Use a different color for each of the following: No Spend, Planned Spend, Unplanned Spend
- **Mood Tracker** - Like a Year in Pixels, but waaay cuter! Write the moods you want to track along the bottom, color code each mood, then fill in the days with the main mood of the day.

Emergency Funds

AKA Peace of Mind

Starter Emergency Fund

If you don't have an Emergency Fund of at least $1000, start here. Resist the temptation to jump straight to paying off debt. You NEED to put a buffer between you and unexpected expenses. Without an emergency fund, you'll be forced to fall back onto the credit card for emergencies. To break that habit, an emergency fund is a necessity.

Start with $1000 at minimum, and work as fast as you can by trimming expenses and increasing your income where you can (sell your unneeded stuff like crazy). Don't make it too big to start or it will take too long to get to the debt payoff and you might lose steam. I've included a worksheet if you want a more precise number, but $1000-$3000 is usually plenty to get you started.

When an unexpected expense comes up, use your Emergency Fund to pay for it. Then refill your Emergency Fund. Then start saving up a **Sinking Fund** for the next time that expense will come around. For more about Sinking Funds see the Savings Goals section.

Your Emergency Fund is NOT a savings account. Don't fall into the trap of not using it and turning to debt instead. **The purpose is to catch unexpected expenses and break the debt habit.** If it helps, think of using it as a debt that you owe to yourself, which you pay back by refilling it.

If used correctly, the Emergency Fund will rise and fall like the tides, more at the start, and less as time goes on and you get control over your money.

Learn more about it at https://debtfreecharts.com/blogs/dfc-blog/emergency-fund

---

Get the Digital Download FREE!

Print off as many copies of your favorites as you need with the Digital Download of this book. It's yours FREE with the purchase of this book. **Find the page in this book with a QR Code to access your FREE download.**

Emergency Fund Worksheet

How much should you save for your Emergency Fund? I have heard recommendations ranging from $500 to a full month's income. The truth is there is no "right" answer. Don't get bogged down in how much, just choose an amount that feels achievable in under 3 months, and get going.

If you'd like a more precise number than that, you can use this sheet to calculate a reasonable amount (but honestly, any amount is better than nothing).

Fill in the amounts for your necessary monthly expenses. This does not include "wants" for the month, only "needs". Imagine you had a job loss for 30 days, what would you absolutely have to pay for during that time? It's probably safe to say you won't be buying clothes or going out for a fancy dinner, you'll be cooking from your pantry and paying the minimum on all your bills. This is a great Starter Emergency Fund amount.

Later, when you've paid off your consumer debt, you can add to your Emergency Fund and get it up to the recommended 3-12 months. But for now, start small, just enough for an emergency month, which should catch most of the typical emergency expenses.

If your budget is so tight it squeaks, and the total you come up with below feels impossible, you can start with half of the total.

Monthly Expenses (Needs only)	Amount
One Month Minimum Expenses Total >	

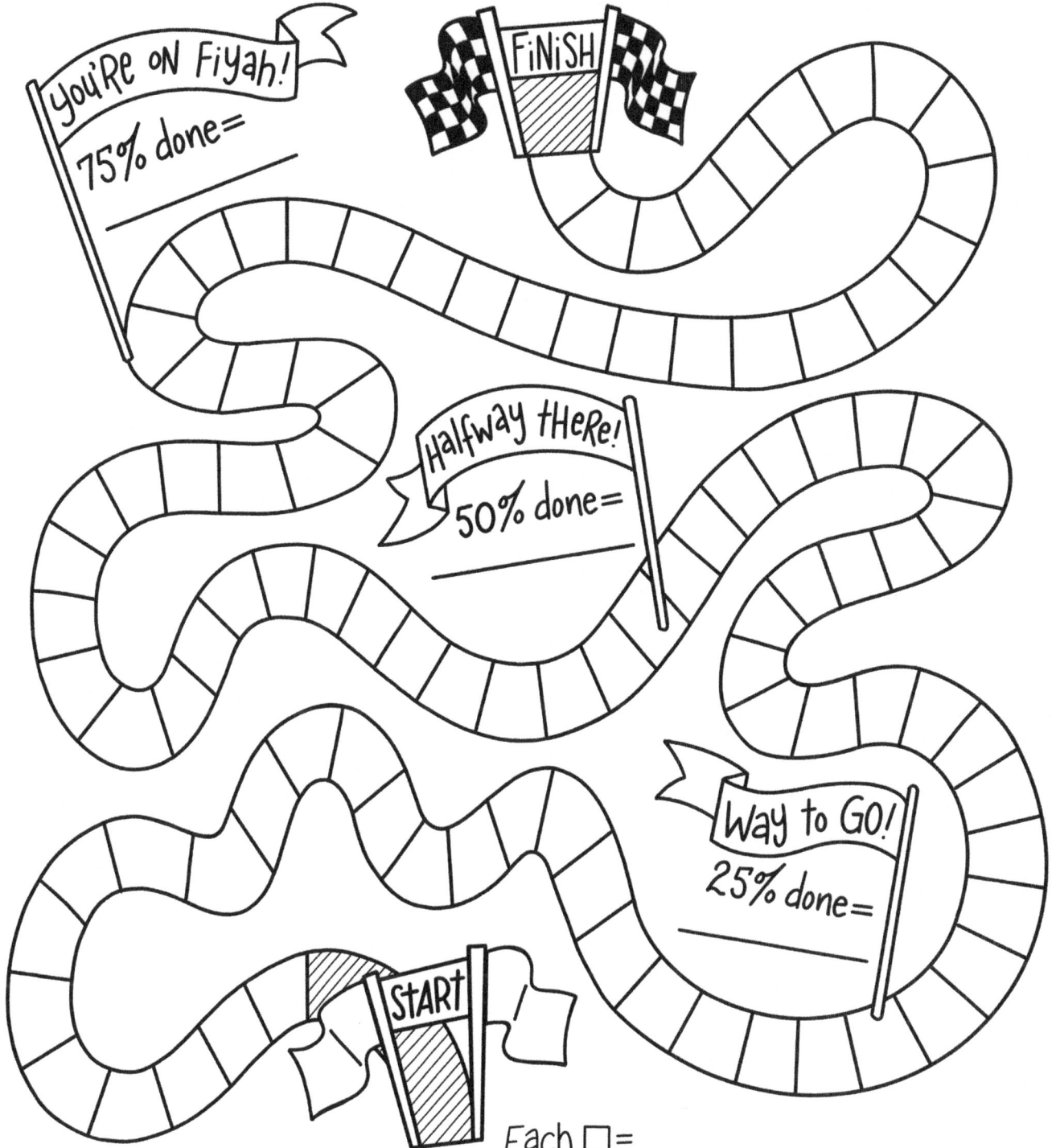

We Saved A *Starter* EMERGENCY Fund

Savings Goal =

You're on Fiyah!

75% done = _____

FINISH

Halfway there!

50% done = _____

Way to GO!

25% done = _____

START

Each ☐ = _____
(there are 100 ☐'s)

Starter Emergency Fund

Goal:	Start Date:	Finish Date:

Use the amount from the worksheet, or choose an amount that feels good to you. You want enough to catch most small emergencies, but not so much that it takes 6 months to save. Be quick about saving this up so you can move on to paying off debt as fast as possible.

Date	Notes	Amount +/-	Balance

STARTER EMERGENCY FUND

EACH SPACE = _____
(There are 100)

Starter Emergency Fund

Goal:	Start Date:	Finish Date:

Use the amount from the worksheet, or choose an amount that feels good to you. You want enough to catch most small emergencies, but not so much that it takes 6 months to save. Be quick about saving this up so you can move on to paying off debt as fast as possible.

Date	Notes	Amount +/-	Balance

EMERGENCY FUND REFILL

EACH SPACE = _____
(There are 100)

Emergency Fund Refill

Goal:	Start Date:	Finish Date:

If you do it right, you WILL use your Emergency Fund at some point. When that happens, you can use this chart to not only refill it, but as a gentle reminder that it's totally normal.

Date	Notes	Amount +/-	Balance

Debt Payoff

The next three trackers are intended as Total Debt trackers. I gave you three options, so you could just choose your favorite for the overall debt, or break up that big number into thirds and use one chart for each third. This is especially useful for large debt totals. Another option is to use each of the three for different groups, like all credit cards or all student loans on one. I still recommend using one of them for the big total, but you can do it however you like.

Choose a tracking chart for the first debt you plan to pay off, filling in the Starting Balance, and the amount each space is worth (divide the total debt by the number of spaces on the chart).

For Debt Payoff trackers **you are tracking your BALANCE**, not your payments. Once a payment clears, check the new balance and then color in your chart accordingly.

If you'd like to track the payment amounts & interest, you can use the Notes field on the Balance Tracker on the back for that.

Once a debt is paid off, write in the date below and celebrate! Be SURE to celebrate ALL your wins. Every little bit matters!

I like to make sure I can color in at least a few spaces each month. If you find you are not able to color in at least one space each month, consider breaking the amount up over several charts. This works very well for big debts.

The most popular debt payoff methods are:
- **Debt Snowball** - Paying debts from smallest balance to largest balance, regardless of interest rate. This gives you faster wins at the beginning which can help you feel like you are making meaningful progress.
- **Debt Avalanche** - Paying debts with the highest interest rates first regardless of balance. While technically smarter when it comes to the math, you'll pay less interest in the long run, this method is harder for many as it can be slow to get the first debts paid off when they have larger balances.
- **Personal Choice** - You choose what to pay off first based on your personal circumstances - I prefer this method because sometimes it's much better to pay family loans first just for the peace of mind, or pay off the loan that irks you the most before the rest.

There is not one "right" way to pay off your debts, but I believe there is one way that is far inferior to all the others. That is to pay off a little of everything every month, not focusing on one. This "a little bit on every loan" can really feel like you aren't making a dent in anything, and I do not recommend it.

Debt Payoff Worksheet

Write down (in any order) all your debts, along with their interest rate, minimum payment, and balance.
In the Payoff Order column, decide what you will pay off first, second, third, etc. by writing in the numbers 1, 2, 3, and so on.
When you pay a debt off, write the payoff date in and celebrate!
When you pay them all off, write the Debt Free Date in at the bottom and throw yourself a party!

Debt	Int Rate	Min Pmt	Start Balance	Payoff Order	Date Paid Off

Debt Free Date	Total Debt

Debt Free Land

Total debt =

You're on Fiyah!
75% done = _____

FINISH

Halfway there!
50% done = _____

Way to GO!
25% done = _____

START

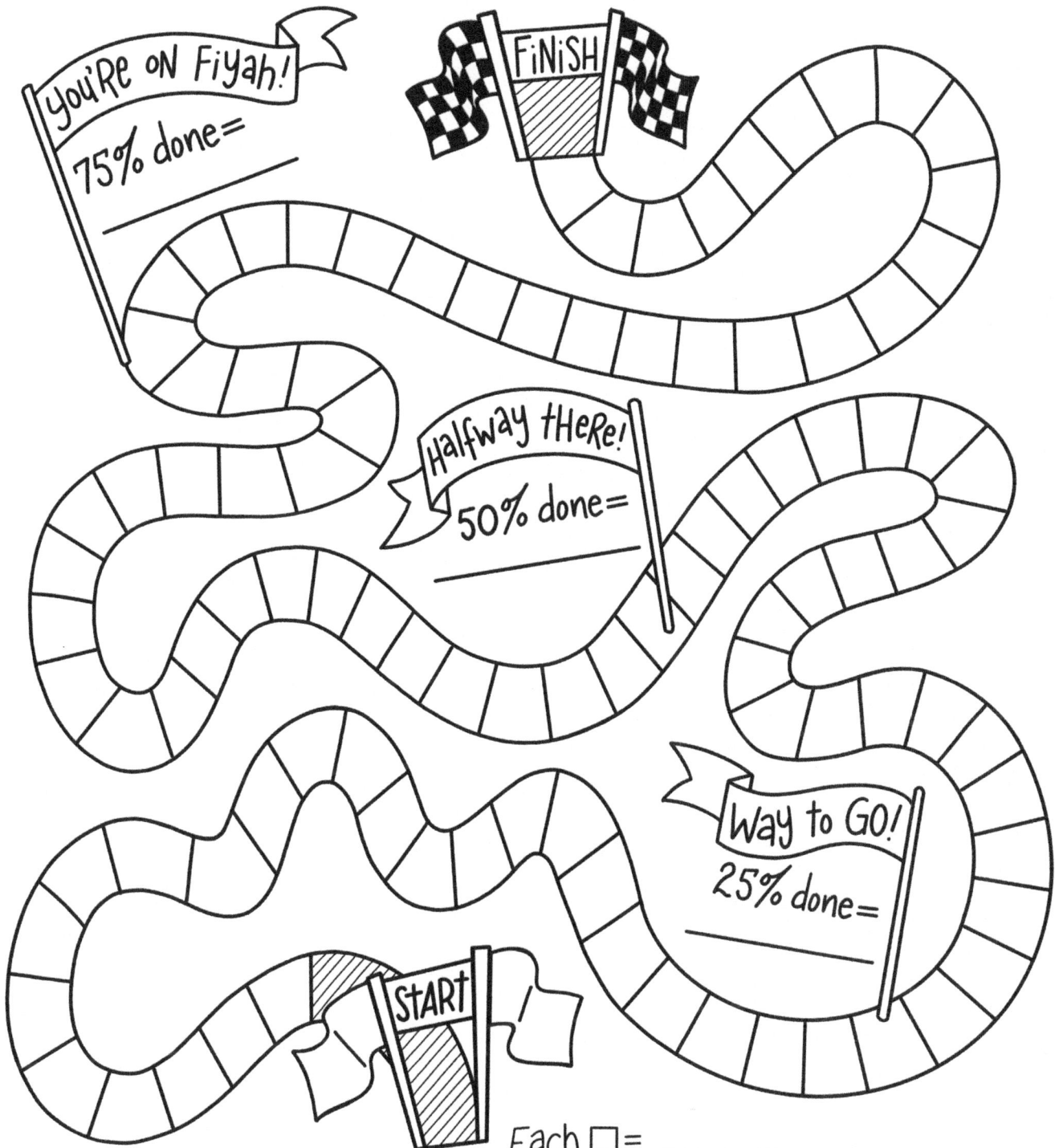

Each ☐ = _____
(there are 100 ☐'s)

Debt Free Land

| Total Starting Debt: | Start Date: | Finish Date: |

This fun Game tracker has 100 spaces to fill in. Use it for your total debt payoff goal, or break up your total into smaller pieces and use one chart for each piece. So if you owe a total of $20,000, you could make four charts of $5000 each.
This is designed to rack your Balance. If you'd like to track the payment amounts & interest, you can use the Notes field for that.

Date	Notes	Amount +/-	Balance

WE'RE DEBT FREE!

TOTAL DEBT : _____   EACH SPACE = _____

(There are 100)

We're Debt Free

Total Starting Debt:		Start Date:		Finish Date:	

This chunky lettered tracker has 100 spaces to fill in. Use it for your total debt payoff goal, or break up your total into smaller pieces and use one chart for each piece. So if you owe a total of $20,000, you could make four charts of $5000 each.
This is designed to rack your Balance. If you'd like to track the payment amounts & interest, you can use the Notes field for that.

Date	Notes	Amount +/-	Balance

DEBTRIS

LEVEL 4

LEVEL 3

LEVEL 2

LEVEL 1

TOTAL DEBT

START DATE

FINISH

EACH PIECE =

(THERE ARE 200 PIECES)

EACH LEVEL =

Debtris Game

This game has 200 pieces, broken into four levels of 50 pieces each. Especially useful for larger balances as you get to color pieces more often. This is designed to rack your Balance. If you'd like to track the payment amounts & interest, you can use the Notes field for that.

Date	Notes	Amount +/-	Balance

We Paid OFF the Credit Card

Starting Balance =

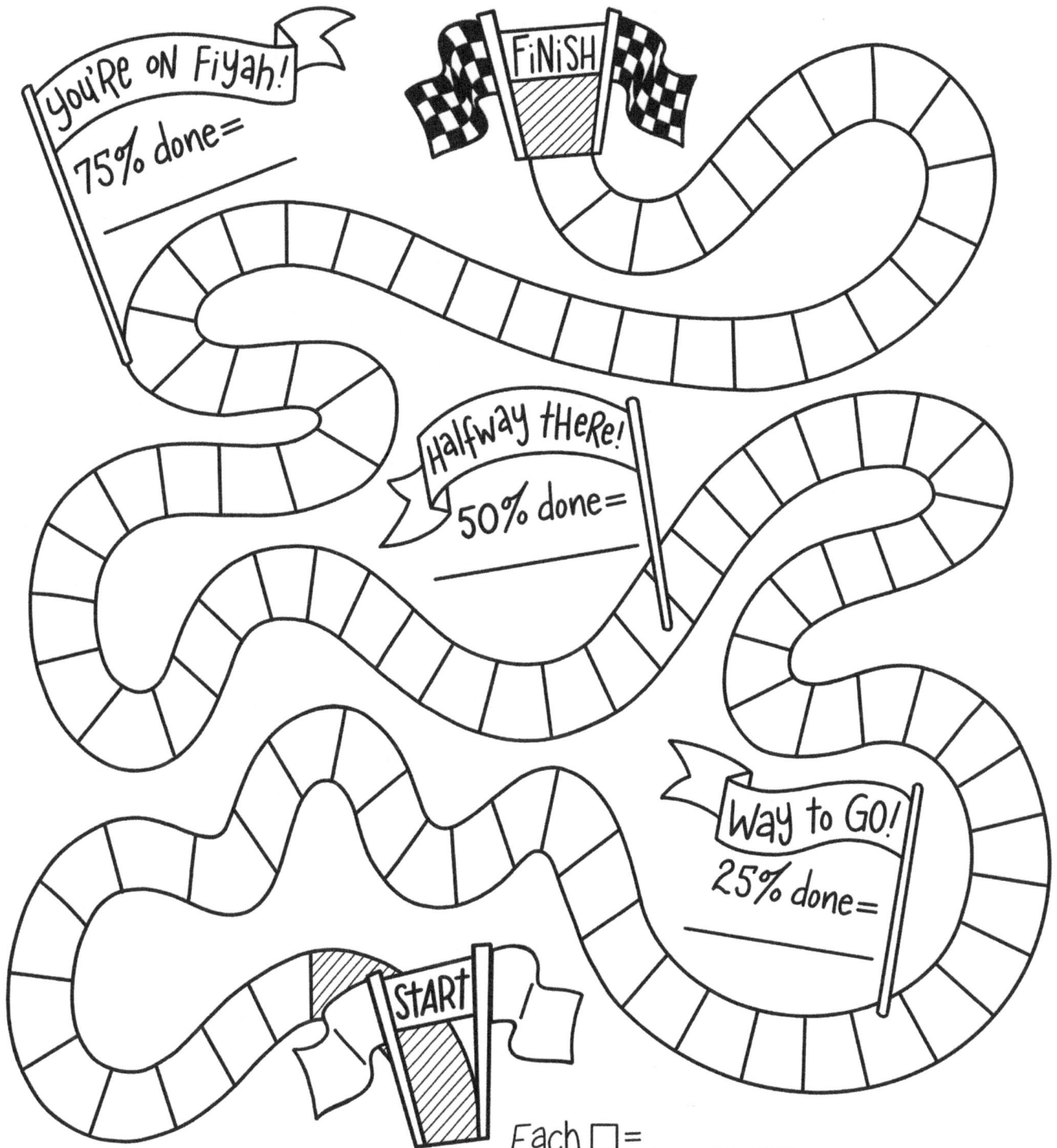

You're on Fiyah!
75% done= _____

FINISH

Halfway there!
50% done= _____

Way to GO!
25% done= _____

START

Each □ = _____
(there are 100 □'s)

Credit Card Payoff Game

Starting Debt:		Start Date:	Finish Date:

This game has 100 spaces, broken into fourths by the flag milestone markers. Under the flags you can write in how much is paid off when you reach it, or how much is left to pay off.
This is designed to rack your Balance. If you'd like to track the payment amounts & interest, you can use the Notes field for that.

Date	Notes	Amount +/-	Balance

WE PAID OFF the CReDIT CaRD

Starting Balance = _____

FINISH

You're on Fiyah!
75% done = _____
_____

Halfway there!
50% done = _____
_____

Way to GO!
25% done = _____
_____

START

Each ☐ = _____
(there are 100 ☐'s)

Credit Card Payoff Game

Starting Debt:	Start Date:	Finish Date:

This game has 100 spaces, broken into fourths by the flag milestone markers. Under the flags you can write in how much is paid off when you reach it, or how much is left to pay off.

This is designed to rack your Balance. If you'd like to track the payment amounts & interest, you can use the Notes field for that.

Date	Notes	Amount +/-	Balance

STEP BY STEP

GOAL:

EACH STEP = _____
(THERE ARE 100)

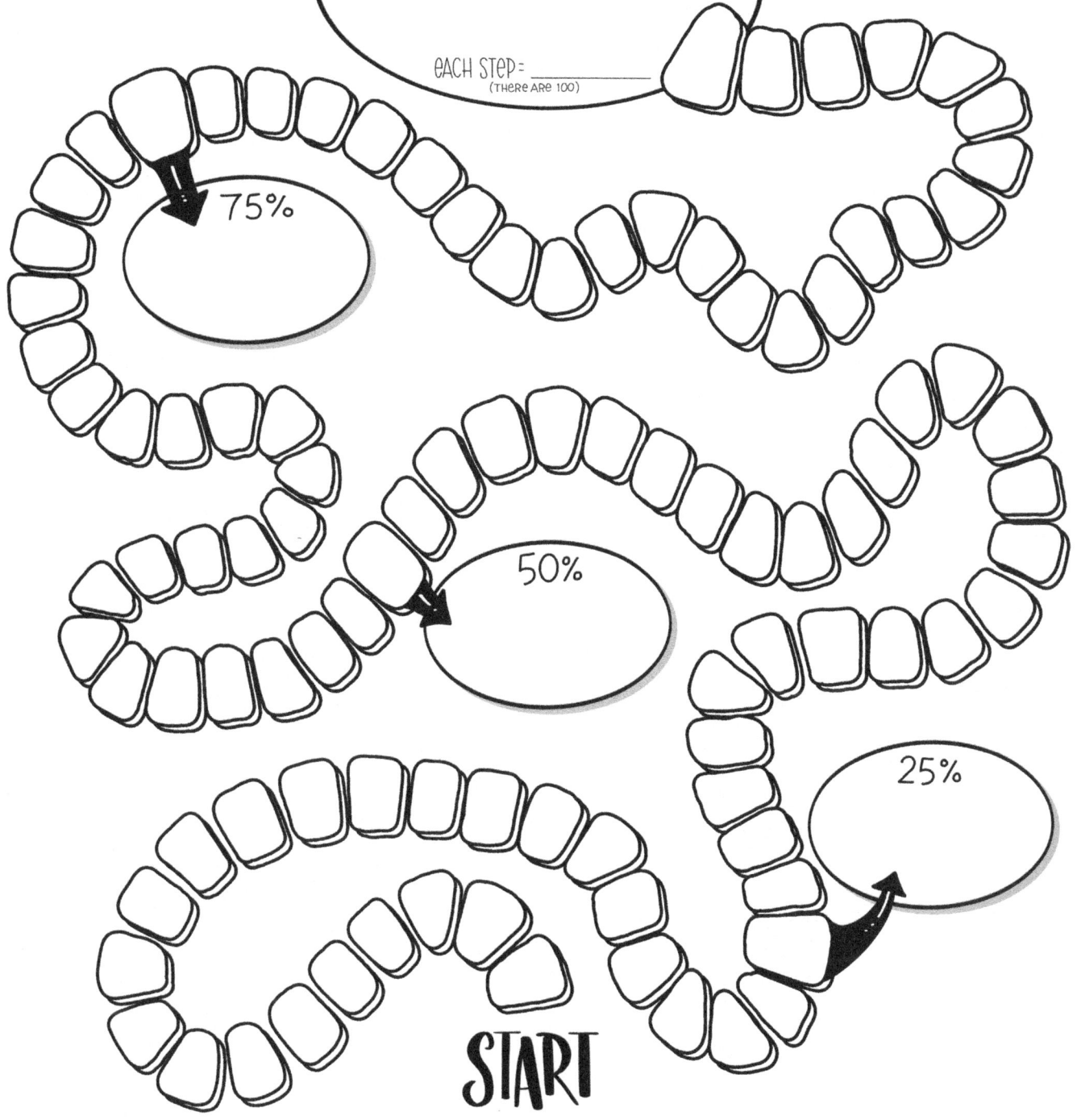

75%

50%

25%

START

Step by Step Game

Starting Debt:		Start Date:	Finish Date:

This game has 100 spaces, broken into fourths by the milestone markers. You can count up or down, write in how much is paid off when you reach a milestone, or how much is left to pay off.
This is designed to rack your Balance. If you'd like to track the payment amounts & interest, you can use the Notes field for that.

Date	Notes	Amount +/-	Balance

[ ] IS PAID OFF!

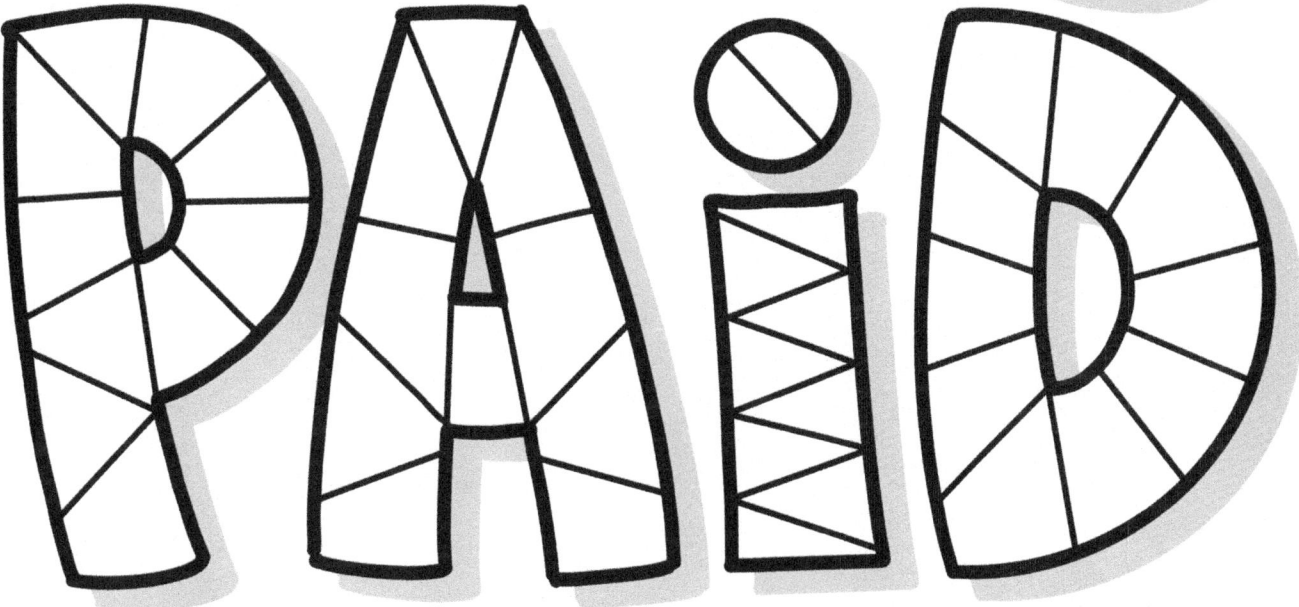

EACH SPACE = _____
(There are 100)

Is Paid Off!

Starting Debt: Start Date: Finish Date:

This tracker has 100 spaces to fill in as you pay off your debt. Each letter is 10 spaces and is 1/10th of the total amount so you can see easily how far your are toward your goal. Divide your debt by 100 to get the amount for each space. Write the name and amount of the debt in the large square. This is designed to rack your Balance. If you'd like to track the payment amounts & interest, you can use the Notes field for that.

Date	Notes	Amount +/-	Balance

is PAiD OFF!

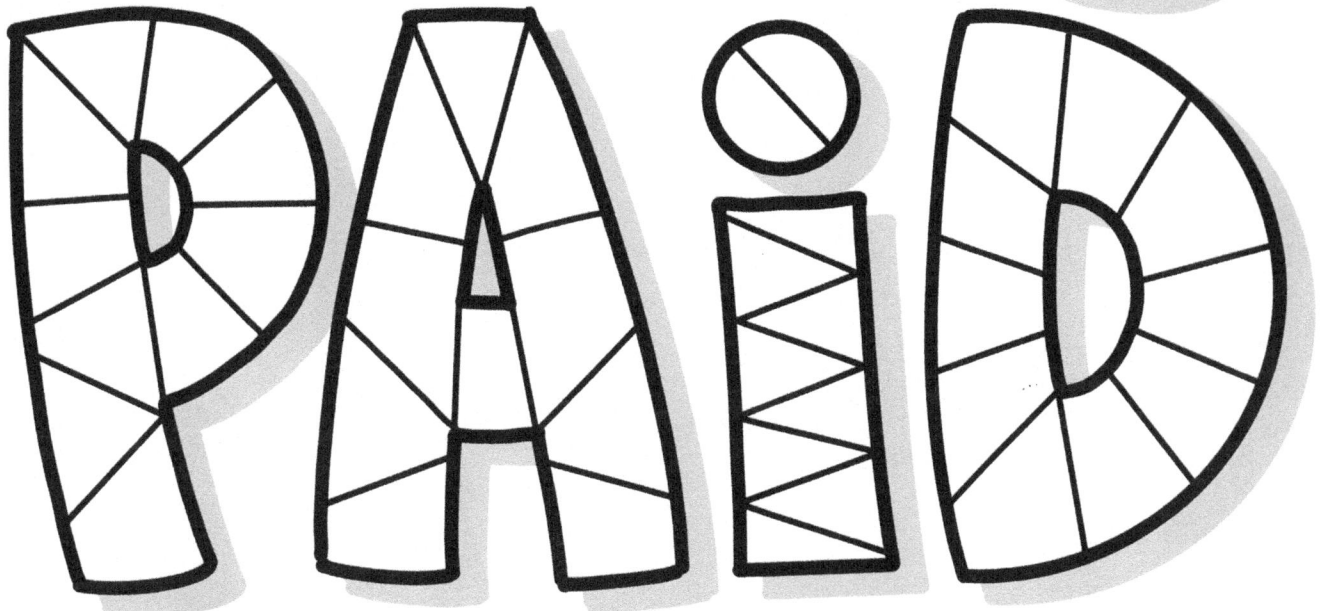

EACH SPACE = _____
(There are 100)

Is Paid Off!

Starting Debt: Start Date: Finish Date:

This tracker has 100 spaces to fill in as you pay off your debt. Each letter is 10 spaces and is 1/10th of the total amount so you can see easily how far your are toward your goal. Divide your debt by 100 to get the amount for each space. Write the name and amount of the debt in the large square. This is designed to rack your Balance. If you'd like to track the payment amounts & interest, you can use the Notes field for that.

Date	Notes	Amount +/-	Balance

We Paid OFF the CAR LOAN

Starting Balance =

You're on Fiyah!

75% done = _____

FINISH

Halfway there!

50% done = _____

Way to GO!

25% done = _____

START

Each ☐ = _____
(there are 100 ☐'s)

Car Loan Payoff Game

Starting Debt:	Start Date:	Finish Date:

This game has 100 spaces, broken into fourths by the flag milestone markers. Under the flags you can write in how much is paid off when you reach it, or how much is left to pay off.

This is designed to rack your Balance. If you'd like to track the payment amounts & interest, you can use the Notes field for that.

Date	Notes	Amount +/-	Balance

Each Space = _____ (there are 100 spaces)

Keep Going

Starting Debt:	Start Date:	Finish Date:

This tracker has 100 spaces to fill in as you pay off your debt. Divide your debt by 100 to get the amount for each space. Write the name an amount of the debt in the large oval.
This is designed to rack your Balance. If you'd like to track the payment amounts & interest, you can use the Notes field for that.

Date	Notes	Amount +/-	Balance

We Paid Off

Starting Balance =

You're on Fiyah!
75% done= _____

FINISH

Halfway there!
50% done= _____

Way to GO!
25% done= _____

START

Each □ = _____
(there are 100 □'s)

We Paid Off:

Starting Debt:	Start Date:	Finish Date:

Write in the name of the debt in the blank space next to We Paid Off. This game has 100 spaces, broken into fourths by the flag milestone markers. Under the flags you can write in how much is paid off when you reach it, or how much is left to pay off.
This is designed to rack your Balance. If you'd like to track the payment amounts & interest, you can use the Notes field for that.

Date	Notes	Amount +/-	Balance

We Paid Off

Starting Balance =

FINISH

You're on Fiyah!

75% done= _____

Halfway there!

50% done= _____

Way to GO!

25% done= _____

START

Each ☐ = _____
(there are 100 ☐'s)

We Paid Off:

Starting Debt: _____ Start Date: _____ Finish Date: _____

Write in the name of the debt in the blank space next to We Paid Off. This game has 100 spaces, broken into fourths by the flag milestone markers. Under the flags you can write in how much is paid off when you reach it, or how much is left to pay off.
This is designed to rack your Balance. If you'd like to track the payment amounts & interest, you can use the Notes field for that.

Date	Notes	Amount +/-	Balance

every little bit counts

EACH SPACE = _____ (THERE ARE 100)

Every Little Bit Counts

Starting Debt:		Start Date:	Finish Date:

This tracker has 100 spaces to fill in as you pay off your debt. Divide your debt by 100 to get the amount for each space.
This is designed to rack your Balance. If you'd like to track the payment amounts & interest, you can use the Notes field for that.

Date	Notes	Amount +/-	Balance

30 DAY Debt Payoff CHALLENGE

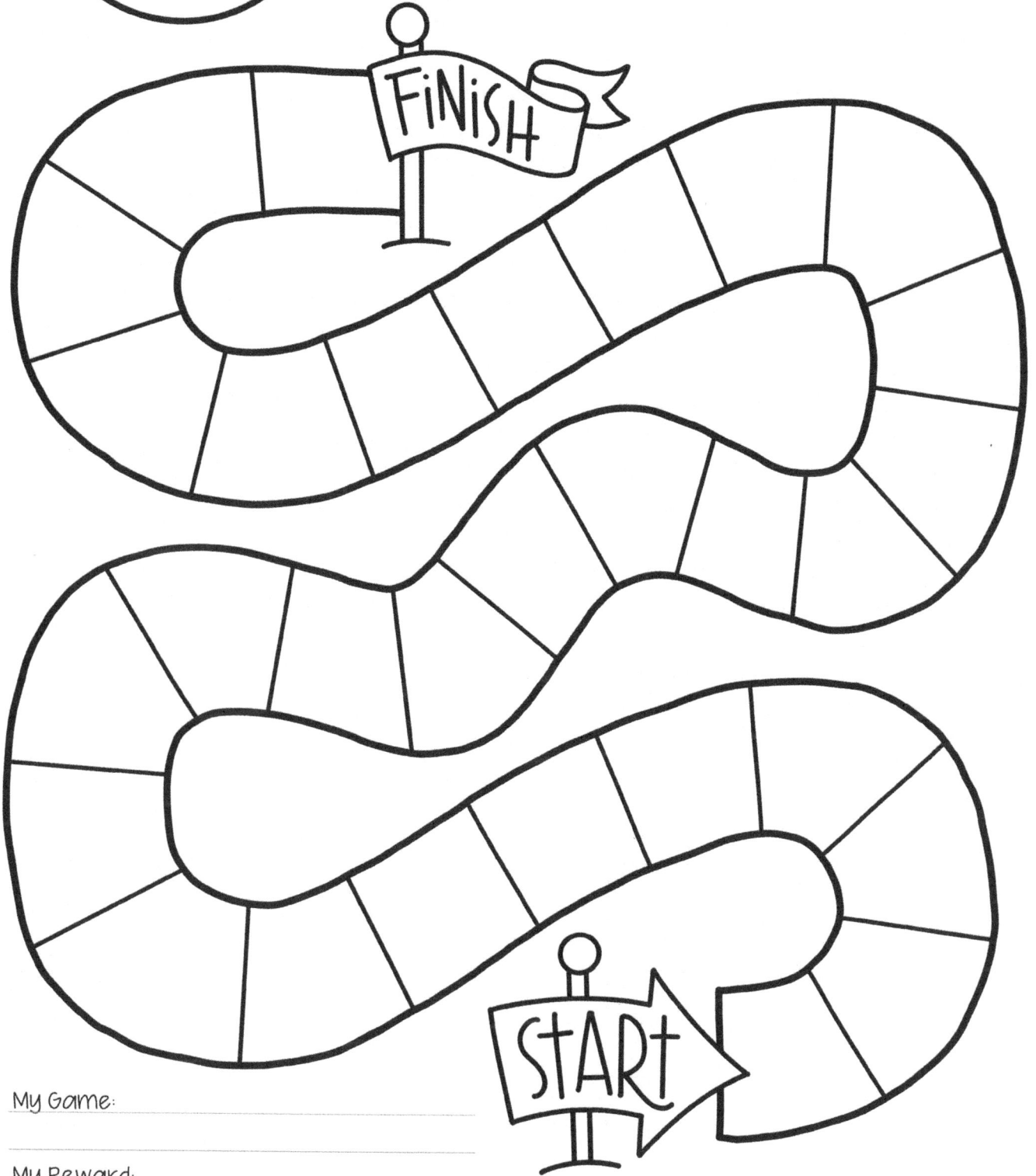

FINISH

START

My Game: _____

My Reward: _____

30 Day Debt Payoff Challenge

The 30-day challenge game is a fun and exciting way to tackle debt and take control of your finances! With at least three different ways to play, you can find the one that works best for you and your unique situation.

And don't forget to celebrate your successes, no matter how small they may seem! Every extra dollar you put towards your debt is a step in the right direction and deserves to be recognized.

The 30-day challenge game offers three different options for paying off debt:

1. Choose a specific amount you want to pay off within 30 days, divide that amount by 30 to get the amount you need to pay off each day, and then color in the corresponding space on a chart for each day you make a payment. By doing this, you can track your progress and see if you can reach your goal by the end of the month.
2. Track how much you shift from spending on unneeded wants towards paying off your debt each day. For instance, if you decide to skip the drive-through and make dinner at home instead, write the amount you would have spent on fast food in that day's space on the chart. At the end of the month, add up all the amounts you saved and see how much extra you paid off. The goal is to shift at least $1 every day towards paying off the debt instead of spending.
3. Do something specific every day to add to your debt payment, such as listing unneeded items for sale, returning purchases you made on impulse, or calling your creditors to get an interest rate reduction on a regular bill. Write what you do each day into each space and how much it added to your debt payoff. Aim to take meaningful action every day. At the end tally up all the extra progress you made and celebrate!

If you have a totally different idea on how to use this 30 Day Challenge, go for it. The most important thing is that you are actively working toward your goal in a way you can measure and see. But most of all have fun with this!

Use the grid below if needed to record your additional debt payoff, the actions you take, or anything else you need.

30 DAY CHALLENGE

GOAL:

30 29 28 27 26 25 24

18 19 20 21 22 23

17 16 15 14 13 12 11 10 9 8 7 6 5 4

LET'S
DO THIS → 1 2 3

30 Day Challenge

The 30-day challenge game is a fun and exciting way to tackle debt and take control of your finances! With three ways to play, you can find the one that works best for you and your unique situation.

And don't forget to celebrate your successes, no matter how small they may seem! Every extra dollar you put towards your goal is a step in the right direction and deserves to be recognized.

The 30-day challenge game offers three different options for saving or paying off debt:

1. Choose a specific amount you want to save or pay off within 30 days, divide that amount by 30 to get the amount you need to pay off or save each day. Color in the corresponding space on the game chart for each day you achieve the daily goal, skipping over the days you don't. Tally up your actual total at the end.
2. Track how much you shift from spending on unneeded wants towards paying off your debt each day. For instance, if you decide to skip the drive-through and make dinner at home instead, write the amount you would have spent on fast food in that day's space on the chart. At the end of the month, add up all the amounts you saved and see how much extra you paid off. The goal is to shift at least $1 every day towards paying off the debt instead of spending.
3. Do something specific every day to add to your savings or debt payment, such as listing unneeded items for sale, returning purchases you made on impulse, or calling your creditors to get an interest rate reduction on a regular bill. Or it could be one action that you need to take every day, like tracking your spending, or not impulse buying. Write what you do each day into each space and how much it added toward your goal. Aim to take meaningful action every day.

If you have a totally different idea on how to use this 30 Day Challenge, go for it. The most important thing is that you are actively working toward your goal in a way you can measure and see. But most of all have fun with this!

Use the grid below if needed to record your actual daily savings/debt payoff amounts, the actions you take, or anything else you need.

Savings Games & Challenges

There are two **30 Day Savings Challenge Games**, and dozens of other **Savings Goal** & **Challenge** trackers.

I did not pre-fill the amounts for the challenges so that they are customizable to your specific situation.

There are several options to customize your challenges:
- Even Amounts - Decide the total for the challenge and divide evenly to get the amount each piece is worth. You can write that amount on each piece if you want. Save that amount daily, or color in several spaces when you save more.
- Randomized - Decide on the total for the challenge and divide into random amounts, writing the numbers on the pieces in any order. Color in one space per day, or several adding up to your total daily savings. This is a bit harder to set up, but can be more fun to color in randomly.
- Save in ascending or descending amounts, day by day. So day 1 is $1, day 2 is $2, and so on.
- Save any amount each day, filling in that day's amount as you go. Add it all up at the end.
- Give yourself a time limit, or not. Some time limit ideas: 30, 50 or 100 days, or a specific end date (like a birthday).
- The **30 Day Savings Challenge Game** is obviously limited to 30 days, but you can customize the rest.

How to use them:
- Write your Savings Goal on the tracker (most have a dedicated space for your goal).
- Decide on your time limit if you want one, and write that on the chart too.
- Determine the amount per space. Write the amounts in the spaces if needed.
- Color in the spaces as you save.
- You can save however you like, in cash, in a dedicated bank account, or in your general account (but keep track of how much you've saved for each savings goal)
- Plan to celebrate with a reward when you finish a challenge (some have a space to write it in to encourage you)

Sinking Fund is a term for savings that are earmarked for a specific expense.
Some common Sinking Funds are Car Repair & Replacement, Christmas Fund, Birthdays, Travel, Property Taxes, etc.
Some Sinking Funds are a specific amount with a known deadline, like Property Taxes, some are a chosen amount with a deadline, like Birthdays, while others are an unknown amount and deadline like Car Repair.

Savings Goals - Sinking Funds Worksheet

Sinking Fund is a term for savings that are earmarked for a specific, known upcoming expense.

Some common Sinking Funds are:

Car Repair & Replacement, Christmas Fund, Birthdays, Travel, Property Taxes, Insurance, School expenses, and so on.

Some Sinking Funds are a specific amount with a known deadline, like Property Taxes, some are a chosen amount with a deadline, like Birthdays, while others are an unknown amount and deadline like Car Repair.

Divide the Amount Needed by the Months to Save to get the Amount per Month you need to add to your savings.

Set up a Savings Chart for each Sinking Fund/Savings Goal, and start saving!

Savings Goal/Sinking Fund	Deadline	Amount Needed	Months to Save	Amount per Month	Date Started	Date Finished

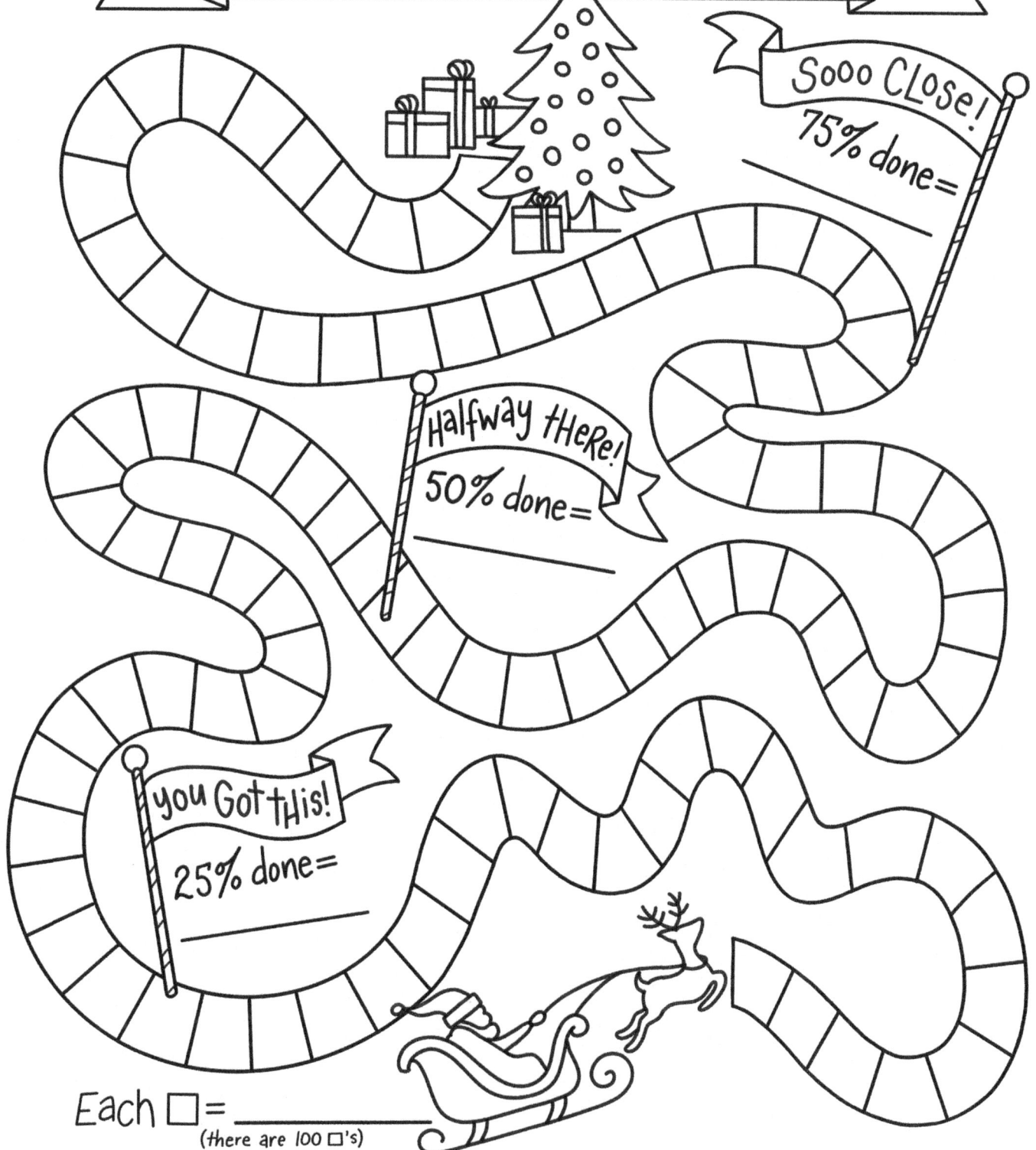

Debt FREE Christmas

GOAL =

Sooo CLOSE!
75% done = _____

Halfway there!
50% done = _____

you Got this!
25% done = _____

Each □ = _____
(there are 100 □'s)

Debt Free Christmas

Savings Goal: _____   Start Date: _____   Finish Date: _____

This game has 100 spaces, broken into fourths by the flag milestone markers. Under the flags you can write in how much is saved when you reach it, or how much is left to save.

Date	Notes	Amount +/-	Balance

CHRISTMAS

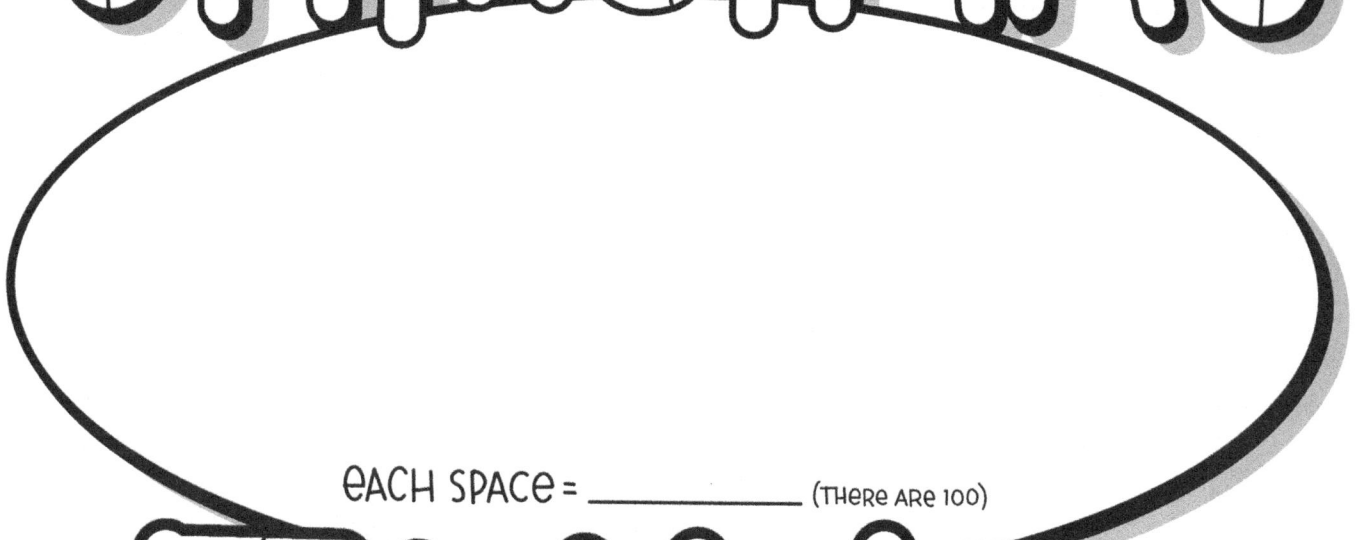

EACH SPACE = _____ (THERE ARE 100)

FUND

Christmas Fund

Savings Goal:		Start Date:		Finish Date:

This tracker has 100 spaces to fill in as you save your Christmas Fund. Divide your goal by 100 to get the amount for each space. Write in the specifics of what you are saving for in the large oval, like Gifts, Travel, etc.

Date	Notes	Amount +/-	Balance

100 Doodles 'till Christmas

Each 🎁 =

(There are 100)

100 Doodles 'till Christmas

Savings Goal: Start Date: Finish Date:

This tracker has 100 doodles to color in as you save. Divide your debt by 100 to get the amount for each doodle.
It could also be used as a 100 Day Countdown for you or your kids.

Date	Notes	Amount +/-	Balance

Ornaments Savings Challenge

Savings Goal: Start Date: Finish Date:

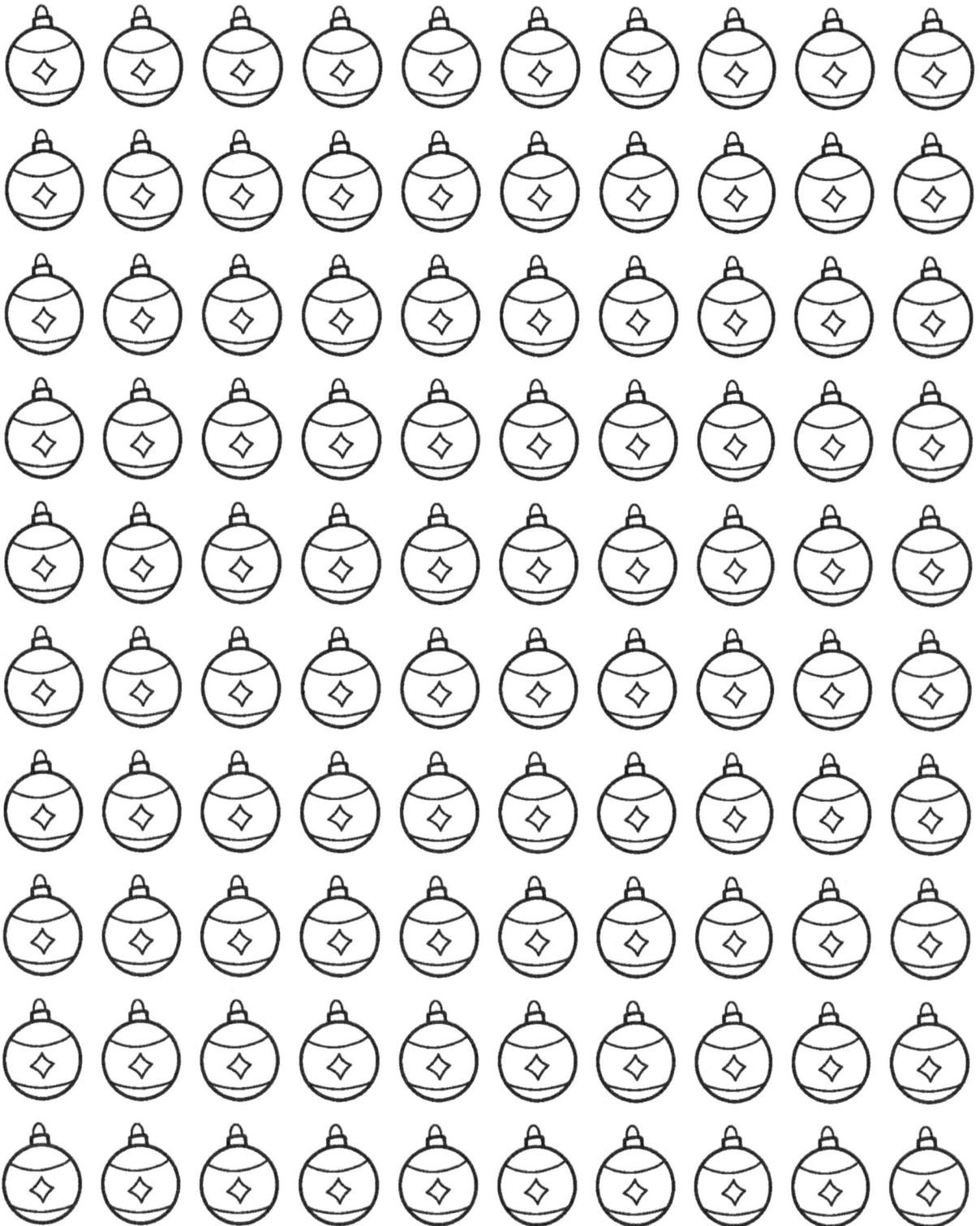

Each Ornament = _____ (There are 100)

Ornaments Savings Challenge

Savings Goal:	Start Date:	Finish Date:

This tracker has 100 Ornaments to fill in as you save for your goal. Divide your debt by 100 to get the amount for each Ornament.

Date	Notes	Amount +/-	Balance

Birthday Land

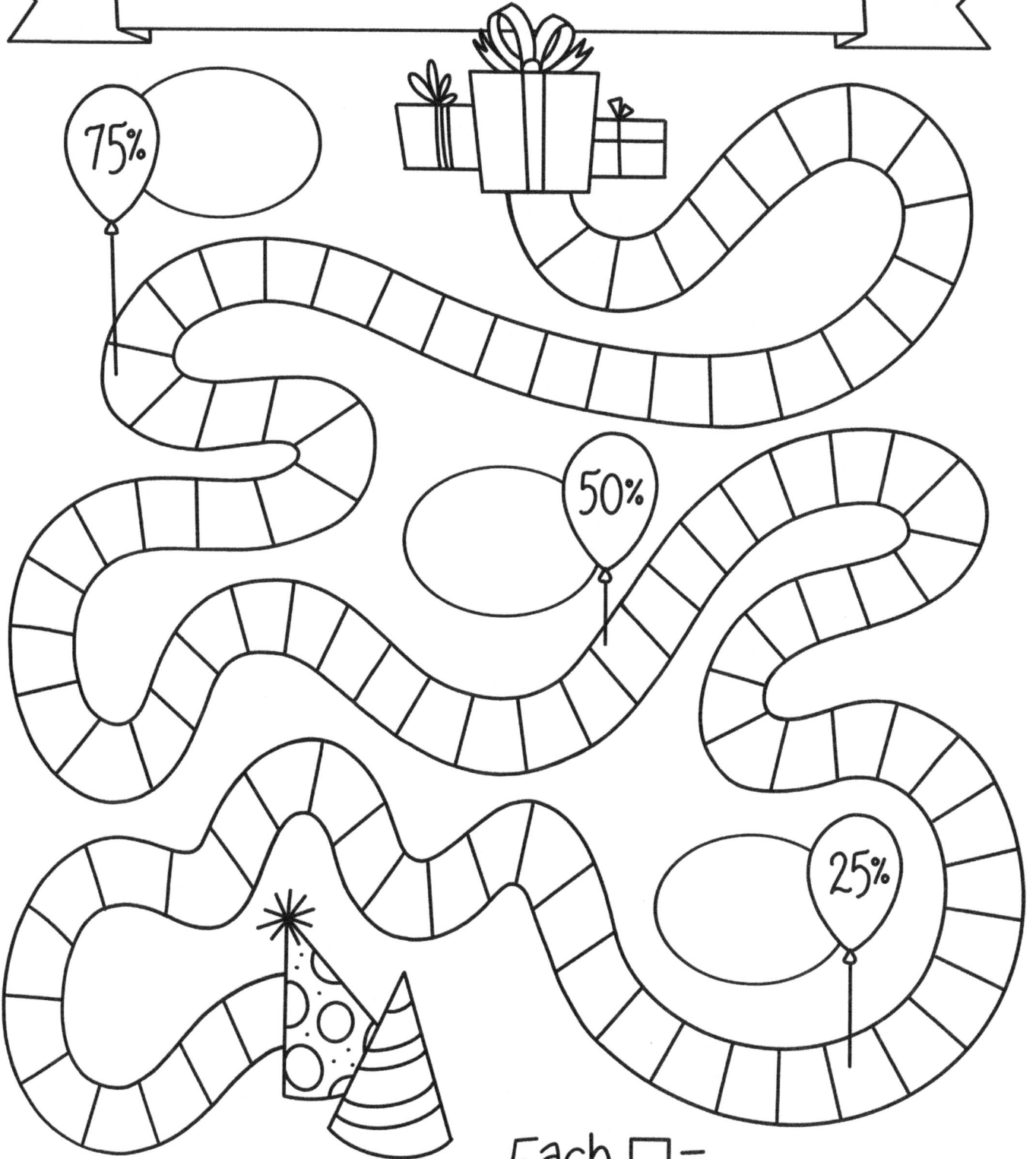

75%

50%

25%

Each ☐ = _____
(there are 100 ☐s)

Birthday Land Game

Savings Goal:		Start Date:	Finish Date:

This game has 100 spaces, broken into fourths by the balloon milestone markers. Under the flags you can write in how much is saved when you reach it, or how much is left to save. Great for saving for birthday presents, parties, even a special birthday trip.

Date	Notes	Amount +/-	Balance

BIRTHDAY

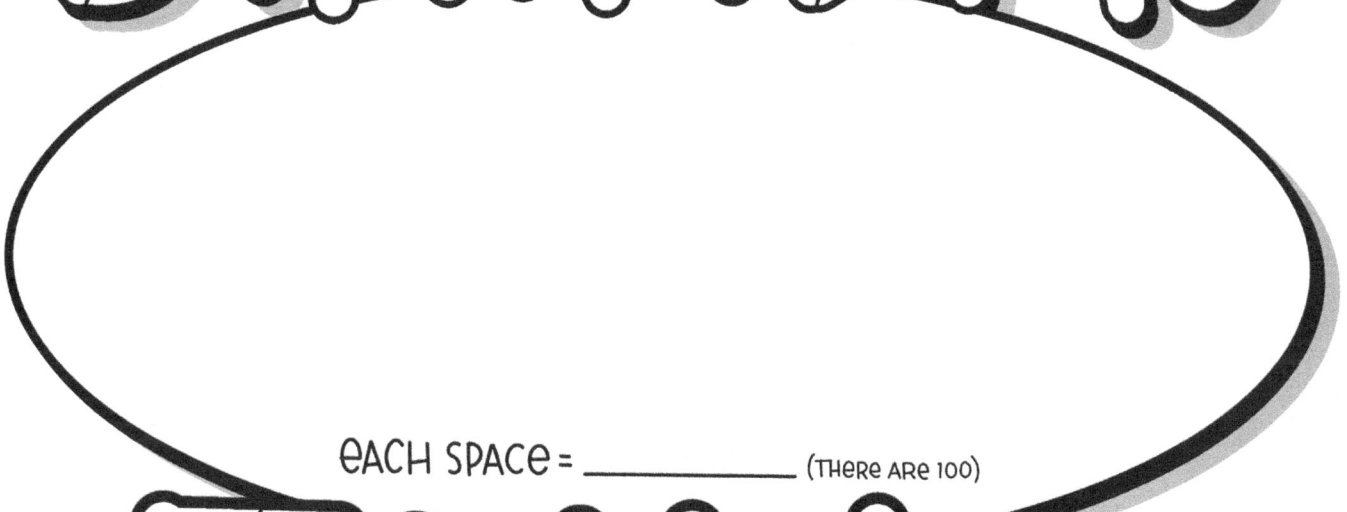

EACH SPACE = _____ (THERE ARE 100)

FUND

Birthday Fund

Savings Goal:		Start Date:	Finish Date:

This tracker has 100 spaces to fill in as you save your Birthday Fund. Divide your goal by 100 to get the amount for each space. Write in the specifics of what you are saving for in the large oval, like who's Birthday, Gifts, Party, etc.

Date	Notes	Amount +/-	Balance

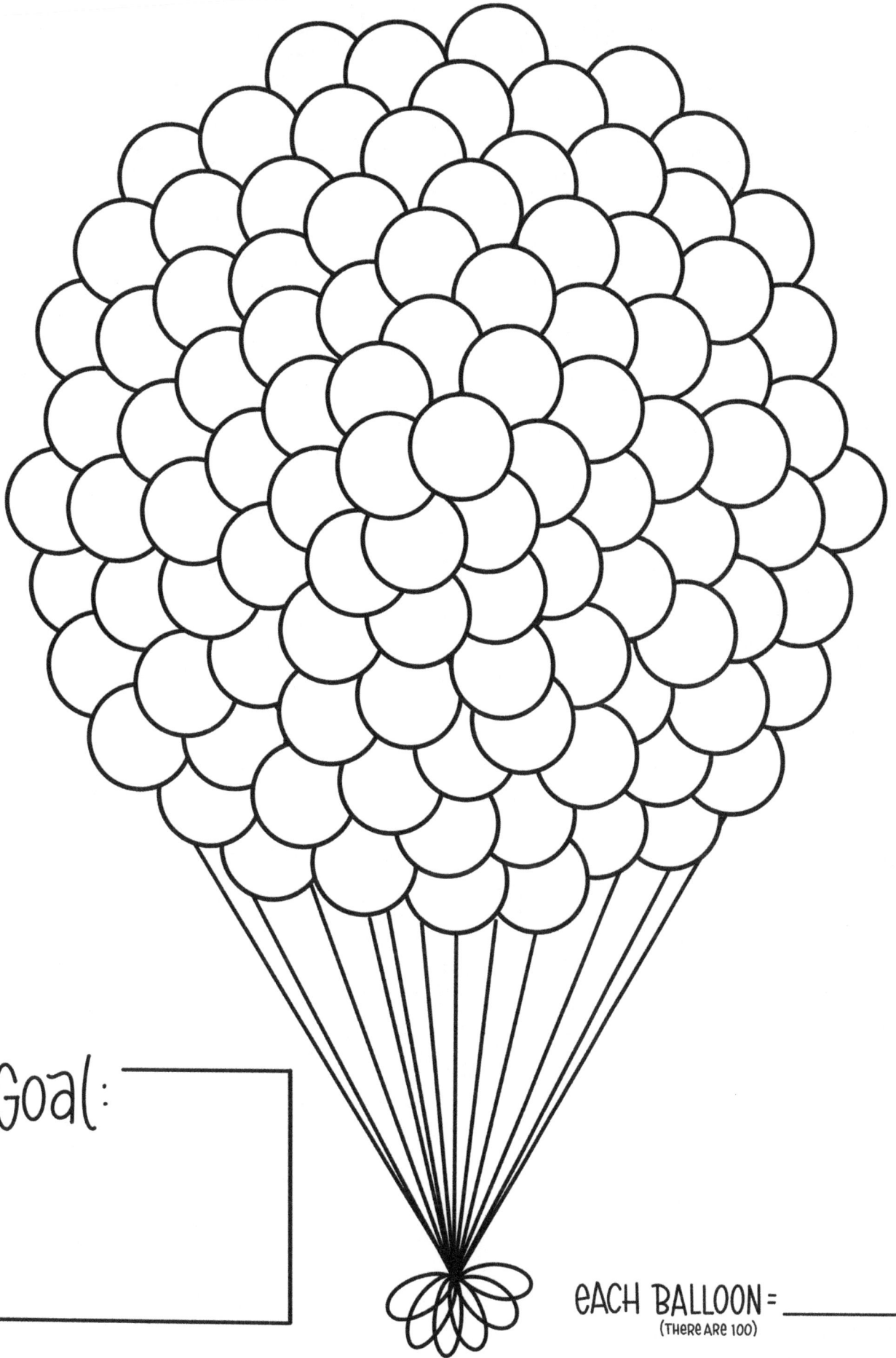

Goal:

EACH BALLOON = _____
(THERE ARE 100)

Balloons Challenge

Savings Goal:	Start Date:	Finish Date:

This tracker has 100 Balloons to fill in as you save toward your goal. Divide your goal by 100 to get the amount for each Balloon.
Write in the specifics of what you are saving for in the Goal space.

Date	Notes	Amount +/-	Balance

Cupcakes Savings Challenge

Savings Goal: Start Date: Finish Date:

Each Cupcake = _____ (There are 100)

Cupcakes Savings Challenge

| Savings Goal: | | Start Date: | | Finish Date: | |

This tracker has 100 Cupcake doodles to fill in as you save. Divide your goal by 100 to get the amount for each Cupcake.

Date	Notes	Amount +/-	Balance

eACH SPACE = _____ (THere are 100)

TRAVEL
FUND

Travel Fund

| Savings Goal: | Start Date: | Finish Date: |

This tracker has 100 spaces to fill in as you save your Travel Fund. Divide your goal by 100 to get the amount for each space.
Write in the specifics of what you are saving for in the large oval, like where you are going and when.

Date	Notes	Amount +/-	Balance

Travel Savings Challenge

Savings Goal: _____   Start Date: _____   Finish Date: _____

Each Doodle = _____ (There are 100)

Travel Savings Challenge

Savings Goal: Start Date: Finish Date:

This tracker has 100 Travel doodles to fill in as you save Divide your goal by 100 to get the amount for each doodle.

Date	Notes	Amount +/-	Balance

Sunny Savings Challenge

Savings Goal: _____   Start Date: _____   Finish Date: _____

Each Sun = _____ (There are 100)

Sunny Savings Challenge

| Savings Goal: | | Start Date: | | Finish Date: | |

This tracker has 100 Summer Suns to fill in as you save Divide your goal by 100 to get the amount for each Sun.

Date	Notes	Amount +/-	Balance

SAVINGS CHALLENGE

GOAL: _____

FINISH

START

EACH FLOWER = _____
(THERE ARE 50)

Flowers Savings Challenge

Savings Goal:		Start Date:	Finish Date:

This tracker has 50 Flower doodle to fill in as you save Divide your goal by 50 to get the amount for each Flower.

Date	Notes	Amount +/-	Balance

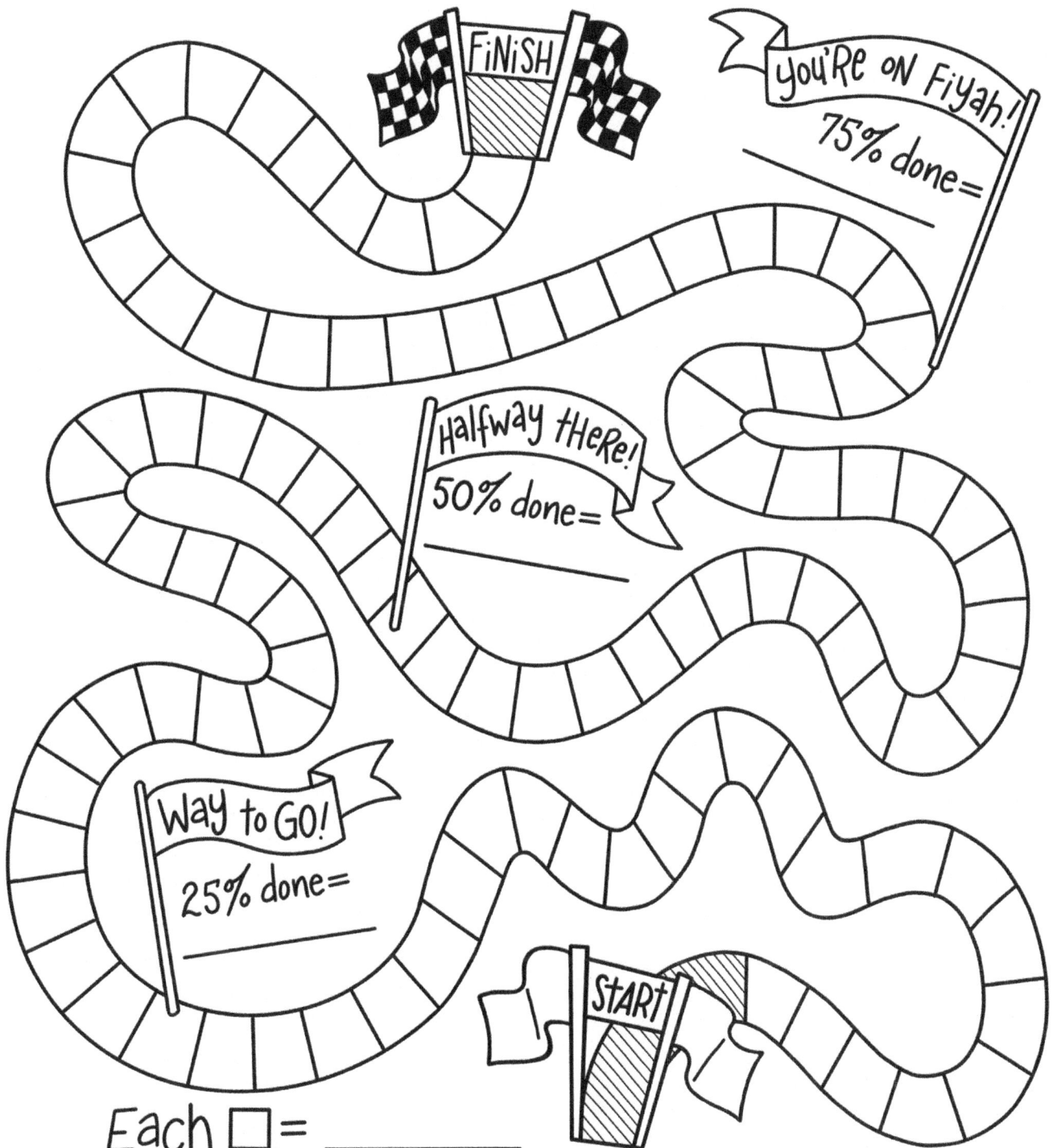

Savings Goal

Goal =

FINISH

you're on Fiyah!
75% done = _____

Halfway there!
50% done = _____

Way to GO!
25% done = _____

START

Each ☐ = _____
(there are 100 ☐'s)

Savings Goal Game

Savings Goal:		Start Date:	Finish Date:

This game has 100 spaces, broken into fourths by the flag milestone markers. Under the flags you can write in how much is saved when you reach it, or how much is left to save.

Date	Notes	Amount +/-	Balance

Leaves Savings Challenge

Goal:

Start Date:

Finish Date:

Each Leaf = _____
(There are 100)

Leaves Savings Challenge

Savings Goal:	Start Date:	Finish Date:

This tracker has 100 Leaves to fill in as you save Divide your goal by 100 to get the amount for each Leaf.

Date	Notes	Amount +/-	Balance

SAVINGS GOAL

EACH SPACE = _____

(There are 100)

Savings Goal Challenge

Savings Goal:	Start Date:	Finish Date:

This tracker has 100 spaces to fill in as you save your goal. Divide your goal by 100 to get the amount for each space.
Write in the specifics of what you are saving for in the large oval.

Date	Notes	Amount +/-	Balance

Buckaroo Challenge

| Savings Goal: | Start Date: | Finish Date: |

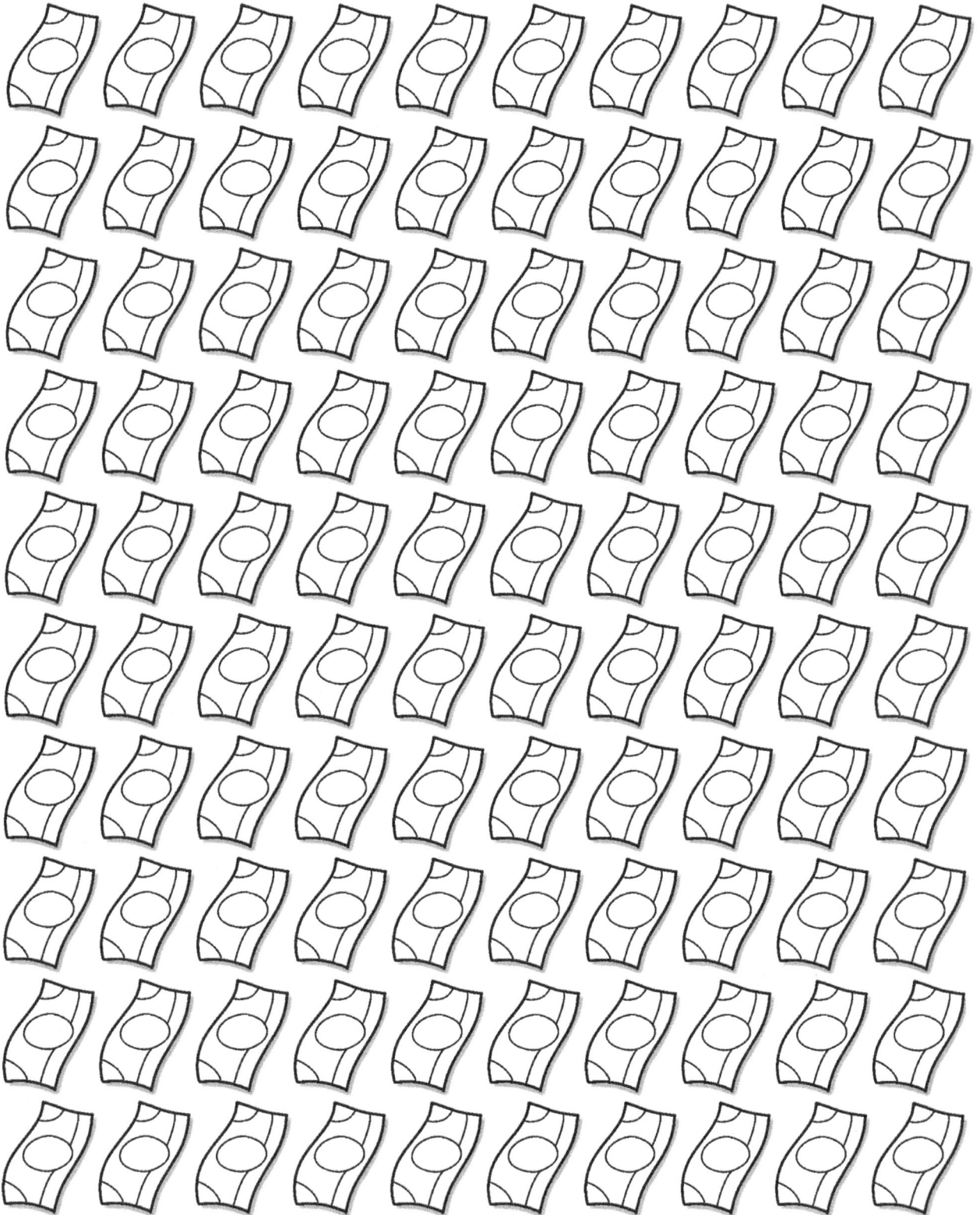

Each Bill = _____ (There are 100)

Buckaroo Challenge

This tracker has 100 Buckaroos (currency notes) to fill in as you save. Divide your goal by 100 to get the amount for each Buckaroo.

Date	Notes	Amount +/-	Balance

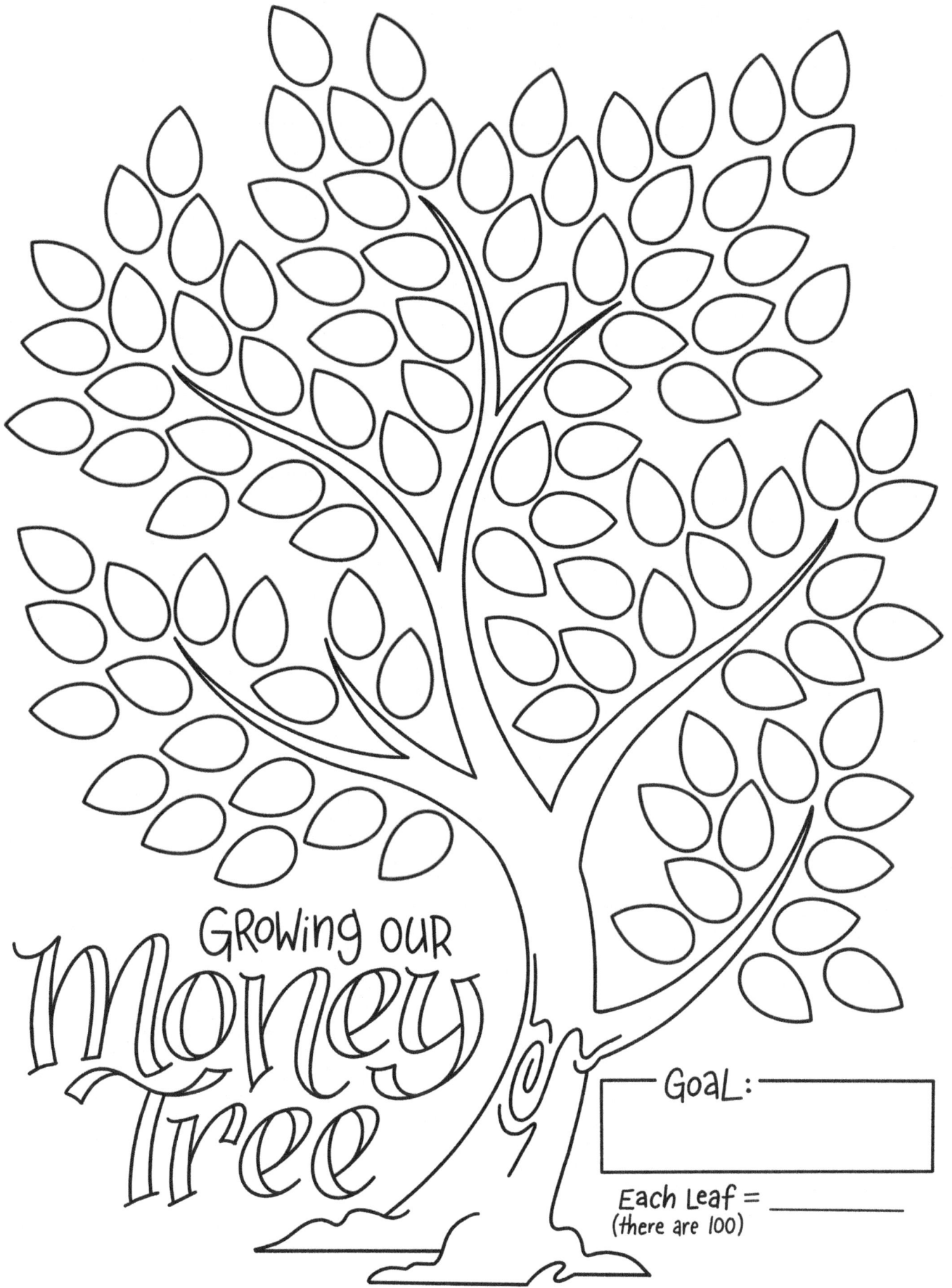

GROWING OUR
Money
Tree

GOAL: _____

Each Leaf = _____
(there are 100)

Money Tree Challenge

Savings Goal:	Start Date:	Finish Date:

This tracker has 100 leaves. Divide your goal amount by 100 to get the amount for each leaf. This one is beautiful colored in with lots of similar colors, like fall leaves from yellow to red, or summer leaves in all shades of green, or in several variants of your favorite colors, whatever that may be.

Date	Notes	Amount +/-	Balance

UNSTOPPABLE

EACH = _____
(There are 100)

UNSTOPPABLE

Savings Goal:		Start Date:	Finish Date:

This tracker has 100 spaces to fill in as you save or pay off your debt. Divide your goal by 100 to get the amount for each space.

Date	Notes	Amount +/-	Balance

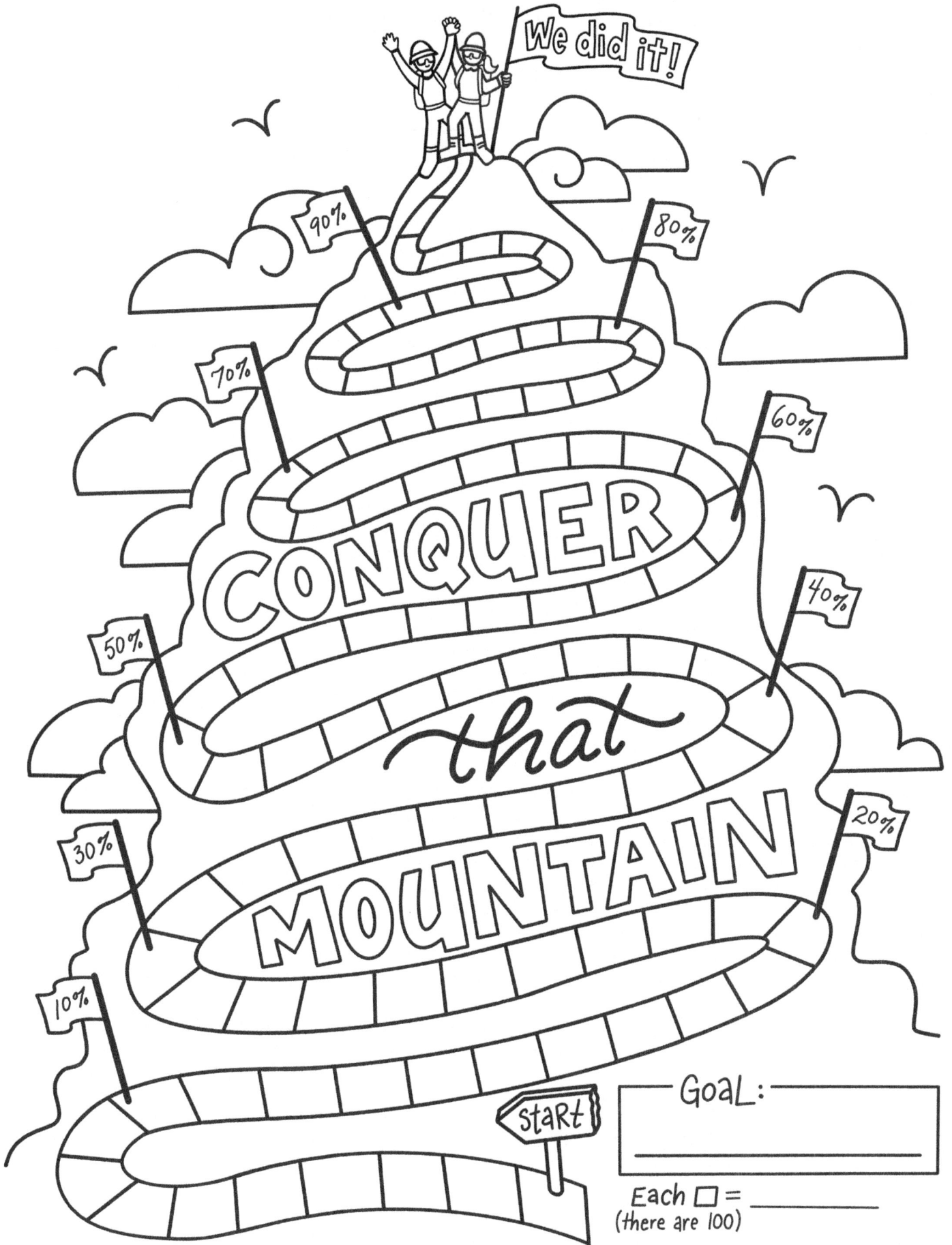

We did it!

CONQUER that MOUNTAIN

90%
80%
70%
60%
50%
40%
30%
20%
10%

Start

Goal: _____

_____

Each ☐ = _____
(there are 100)

Conquer That Mountain Game

Goal:		Start Date:		Finish Date:	

This tracker has 100 spaces to color in as you save, with milestone markers for every 10%.
Divide your goal by 100 to get the amount for each step up the mountain.

Date	Notes	Amount +/-	Balance

SAVINGS CHALLENGE

GOAL: _____

FINISH

START

EACH HEART = _____
(THERE ARE 50)

Hearts Savings Challenge

Savings Goal:		Start Date:		Finish Date:	

This tracker has 50 Hearts to fill in as you save Divide your goal by 50 to get the amount for each Heart
You can also use this to save 1275 by numbering the hearts 1-50, either in order, or randomly.

Date	Notes	Amount +/-	Balance

Succulent Savings Challenge

| Goal: | Start Date: |
| | Finish Date: |

Each Leaf = _____
(There are 100)

Succulent Savings Challenge

| Savings Goal: | Start Date: | Finish Date: |

This tracker has 100 Leaves to fill in as you save Divide your goal by 100 to get the amount for each Leaf.

Date	Notes	Amount +/-	Balance

Cactus Savings Challenge

Savings Goal: _____   Start Date: _____   Finish Date: _____

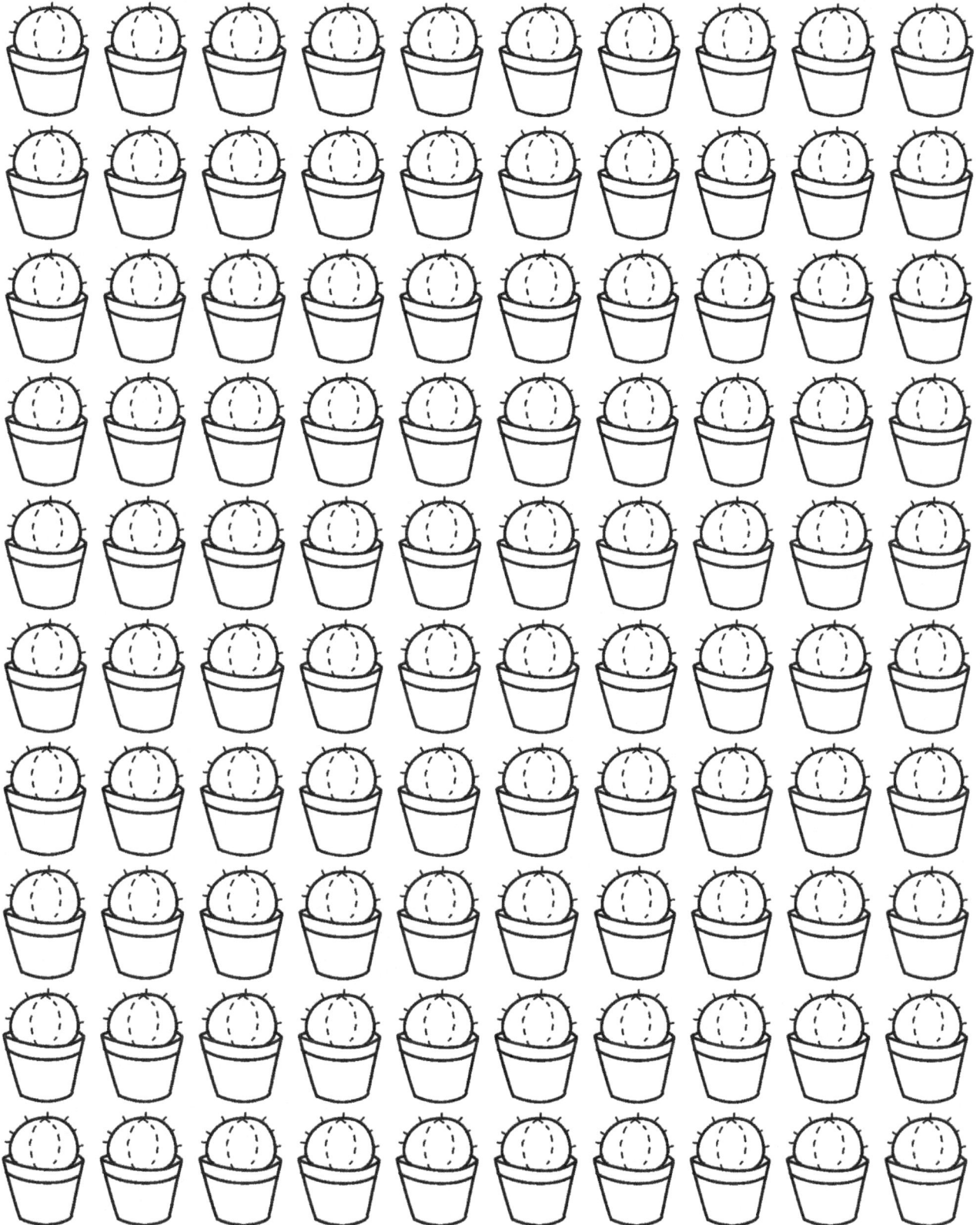

Each Cactus = _____ (There are 100)

Cactus Challenge

Savings Goal:		Start Date:		Finish Date:	

This Challenge has 100 little Cactus in pots. You could even make it 200 by counting the pots and the cactus plants separately. Divide your goal amount by either 100 or 200.

Date	Notes	Amount +/-	Balance

SUPERSAVER

GOAL _____

Each Space = _____ (There are 100)

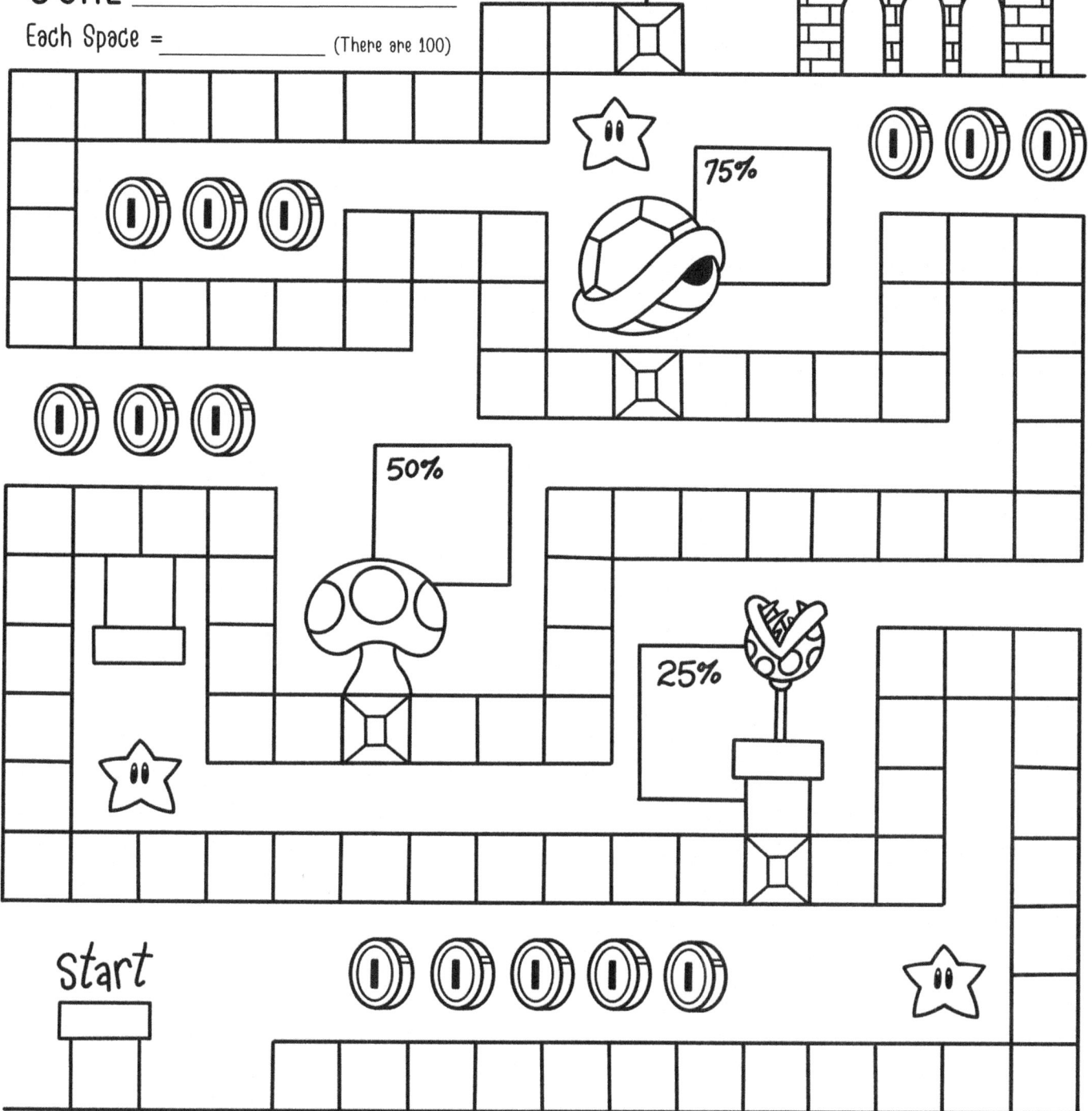

75%

50%

25%

Start

SuperSaver Game

Savings Goal: Start Date: Finish Date:

This game has 100 spaces, broken into fourths by the milestone markers.
Beside the markers you can write in how much is saved when you reach it. Don't forget to celebrate!

Date	Notes	Amount +/-	Balance

CASH STASH

GOAL: _____

FINISH

START

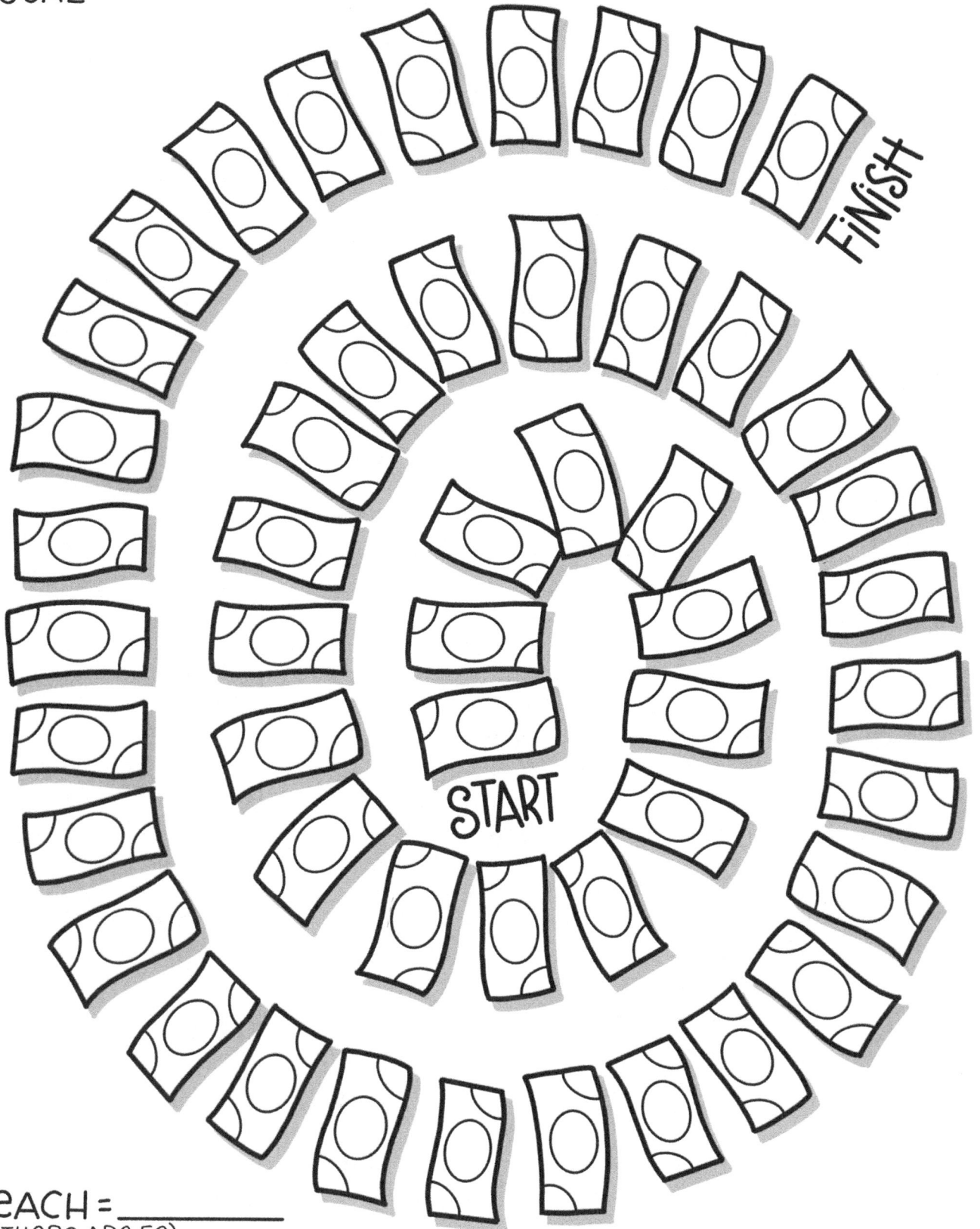

eACH = _____
(THERE ARE 50)

Cash Stash Game

Goal:		Start Date:		Finish Date:

This game has 50 currency notes - Use for Savings or Debt
You can divide up your goal by 50 for even amounts, or use it for a 50 Day Challenge, writing in the amount you save/pay off each day.

Date	Notes	Amount +/-	Balance

CASH STASH

GOAL: _____

FINISH

START

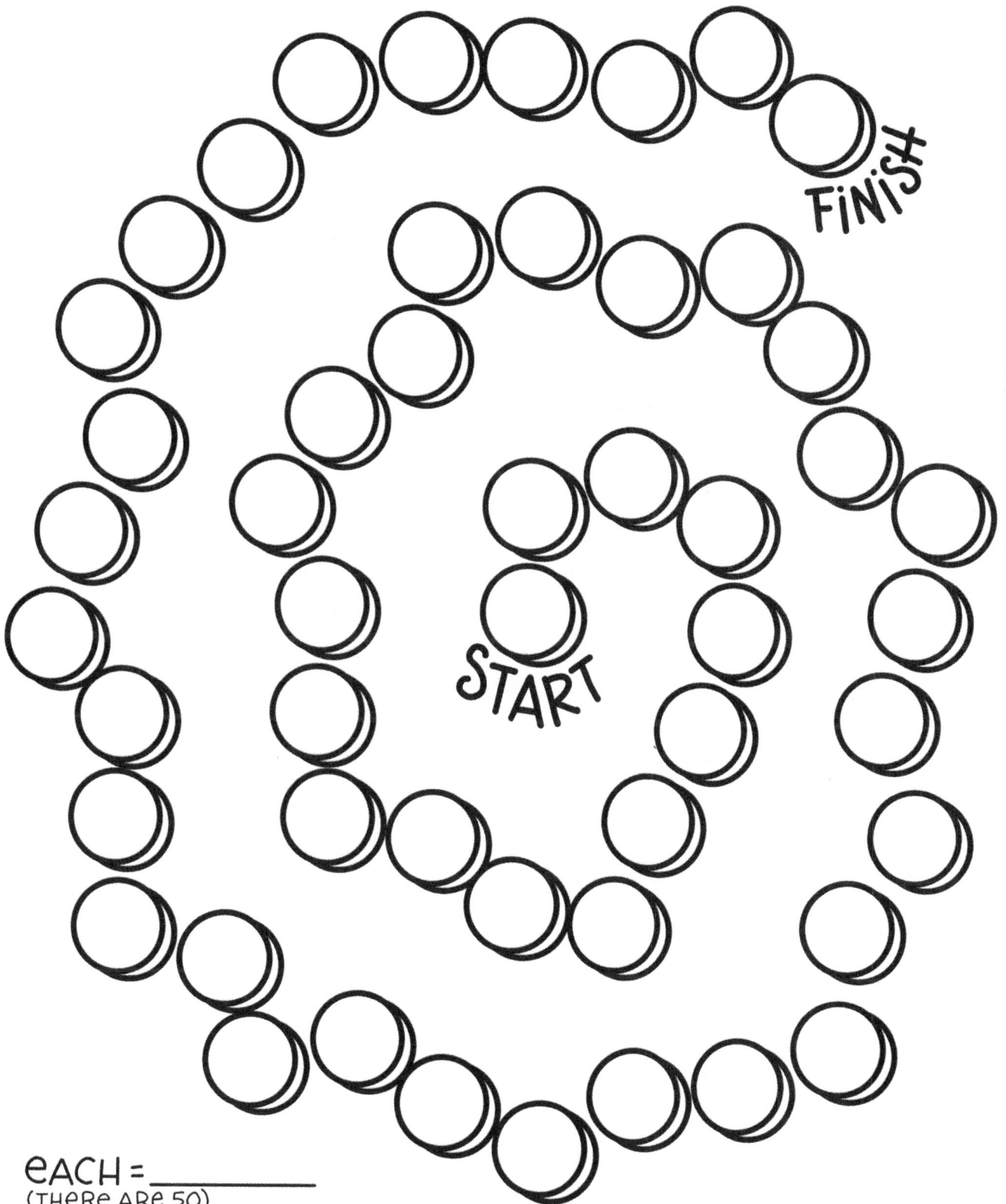

EACH = _____
(THERE ARE 50)

Cash Stash Game

Goal:		Start Date:		Finish Date:	

This game has 50 coins - Use for Savings or Debt
You can divide up your goal by 50 for even amounts, or use it for a 50 Day Challenge, writing in the amount you save/pay off each day.

Date	Notes	Amount +/-	Balance

Stars Savings Challenge

Savings Goal:	Start Date:	Finish Date:

☆ ☆ ☆ ☆ ☆ ☆ ☆ ☆ ☆ ☆

☆ ☆ ☆ ☆ ☆ ☆ ☆ ☆ ☆ ☆

☆ ☆ ☆ ☆ ☆ ☆ ☆ ☆ ☆ ☆

☆ ☆ ☆ ☆ ☆ ☆ ☆ ☆ ☆ ☆

☆ ☆ ☆ ☆ ☆ ☆ ☆ ☆ ☆ ☆

☆ ☆ ☆ ☆ ☆ ☆ ☆ ☆ ☆ ☆

☆ ☆ ☆ ☆ ☆ ☆ ☆ ☆ ☆ ☆

☆ ☆ ☆ ☆ ☆ ☆ ☆ ☆ ☆ ☆

☆ ☆ ☆ ☆ ☆ ☆ ☆ ☆ ☆ ☆

☆ ☆ ☆ ☆ ☆ ☆ ☆ ☆ ☆ ☆

Each Star = _____ (There are 100)

Stars Savings Challenge

Savings Goal:	Start Date:	Finish Date:

This Challenge has 100 Stars. Divide your goal amount by either 100 to get the amount for each Star.

Date	Notes	Amount +/-	Balance

SAVINGS CHALLENGE

GOAL: _____

FINISH

START

EACH LEAF = _____
(THERE ARE 50)

Leafy Savings Challenge Game

Savings Goal:		Start Date:	Finish Date:

This tracker has 50 Leaves to fill in as you save Divide your goal by 50 to get the amount for each Leaf
You can also use this to save 1275 by numbering the hearts 1-50, either in order, or randomly.

Date	Notes	Amount +/-	Balance

100 ENVELOPE CHALLENGE

1	2	3	4	5	6	7	8	9	10
11	12	13	14	15	16	17	18	19	20
21	22	23	24	25	26	27	28	29	30
31	32	33	34	35	36	37	38	39	40
41	42	43	44	45	46	47	48	49	50
51	52	53	54	55	56	57	58	59	60
61	62	63	64	65	66	67	68	69	70
71	72	73	74	75	76	77	78	79	80
81	82	83	84	85	86	87	88	89	90
91	92	93	94	95	96	97	98	99	100

100 Envelope Challenge

There are two 100 Envelope Challenges included in this book.

The first is numbered in the normal way, from 1 to 100 (I didn't include currency symbols so it works all over the world). Saving according to these amounts would mean you'd have 5,050 at the end.

The second one has no amounts filled in, so you can choose custom amounts and write in what you like.

Completing the 100 Envelope Challenge is a fun and effective way to save money.

Here's how to do it using a tracking sheet along with cash and actual envelopes.

1. Get 100 envelopes and label each one with a dollar amount (1-100, or any amounts you choose). Write those same numbers on the tracking sheet if needed.
2. Each day, randomly select one envelope and put the corresponding dollar amount into it. Do this until all envelopes have been filled.
3. As you fill each envelope, mark the corresponding dollar amount on the 100 Envelope Challenge tracking sheet.
4. Once all envelopes have been filled, count the total amount of money saved, write the total in the box at the top of the tracker, and celebrate your accomplishment!

Remember, the key to completing the 100 Envelope Challenge is consistency. Stick to the daily routine and use the tracking sheet to stay motivated and track your progress. Good luck!

Don't want to use real envelopes and cash? No Problem!

The 100 Envelope Challenge can still be done without using cash by using just the 100 Envelope Challenge tracker. Here's how to do it:

1. Each day, use the tracker to randomly select one dollar amount and mark it as "filled".
2. To "fill" the envelope, transfer the corresponding dollar amount into a separate savings account (banks may limit the number of monthly transfers) or simply add it to a designated savings category in your budgeting app or spreadsheet.
3. Repeat this process every day until all 100 dollar amounts have been marked as "filled".
4. At the end of the challenge, count up the total you saved and write it in the box at the top of the tracker.
5. If needed transfer the final total to your savings.

Just using the tracker can make the challenge more convenient and accessible, especially for those who prefer not to use cash or have limited access to physical envelopes. The important thing is to stay consistent and disciplined in saving each day.

100 ENVELOPE CHALLENGE

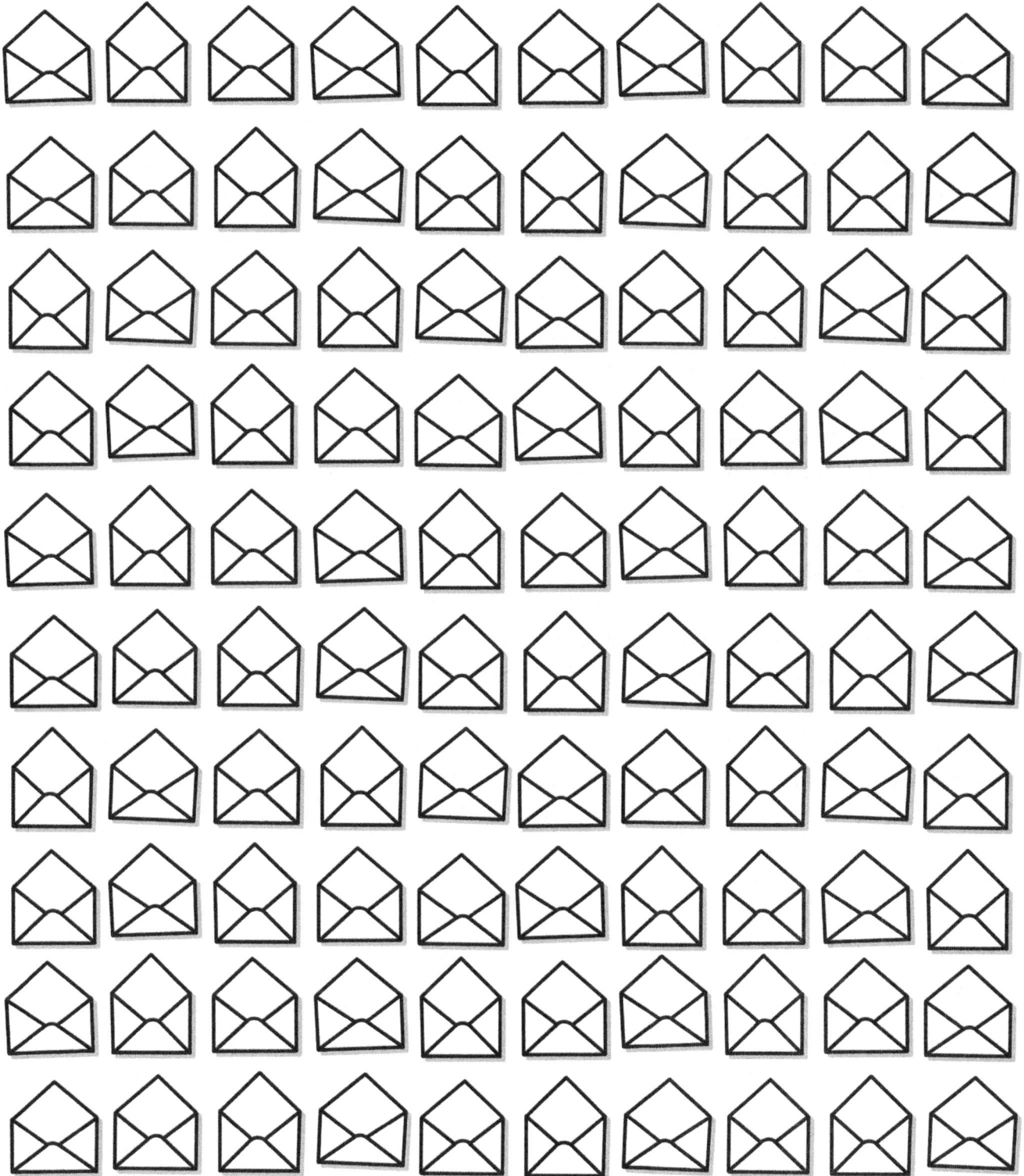

100 Envelope Challenge

There are two 100 Envelope Challenges included in this book.

The first is numbered in the normal way, from 1 to 100 (I didn't include currency symbols so it works all over the world). Saving according to these amounts would mean you'd have 5050 at the end.

The second one has no amounts filled in, so you can choose custom amounts and write in what you like.

Completing the 100 Envelope Challenge is a fun and effective way to save money.

Here's how to do it using a tracking sheet along with cash and actual envelopes.

1. Get 100 envelopes and label each one with a dollar amount (1-100, or any amounts you choose). Write those same numbers on the tracking sheet if needed.
2. Each day, randomly select one envelope and put the corresponding dollar amount into it. Do this until all envelopes have been filled.
3. As you fill each envelope, mark the corresponding dollar amount on the 100 Envelope Challenge tracking sheet.
4. Once all envelopes have been filled, count the total amount of money saved, write the total in the box at the top of the tracker, and celebrate your accomplishment!

Remember, the key to completing the 100 Envelope Challenge is consistency. Stick to the daily routine and use the tracking sheet to stay motivated and track your progress. Good luck!

Don't want to use real envelopes and cash? No Problem!

The 100 Envelope Challenge can still be done without using cash by using just the 100 Envelope Challenge tracker. Here's how to do it:

1. Each day, use the tracker to randomly select one dollar amount and mark it as "filled".
2. To "fill" the envelope, transfer the corresponding dollar amount into a separate savings account, or simply add it to a designated savings category in your budgeting app or spreadsheet.
3. Repeat this process every day until all 100 dollar amounts have been marked as "filled".
4. At the end of the challenge, count up the total you saved and write it in the box at the top of the tracker.

Just using the tracker can make the challenge more convenient and accessible, especially for those who prefer not to use cash or have limited access to physical envelopes. The important thing is to stay consistent and disciplined in saving each day.

SAVINGS CHALLENGE

GOAL: _____

FINISH

START

EACH STAR= _____
(THERE ARE 50 STARS)

Stars Savings Challenge Game

Savings Goal:		Start Date:	Finish Date:

This tracker has 50 Stars to fill in as you save Divide your goal by 50 to get the amount for each Star.
You can also use this to save 1275 by numbering the hearts 1-50, either in order, or randomly.

Date	Notes	Amount +/-	Balance

GROWING OUR GREEN

GOAL: _____

EACH LEAF = _____   START DATE: _____   FINISH DATE: _____
(There are 100)

Growing Our Green

Savings Goal: **Start Date:**   **Finish Date:**

This page has 100 individual leaves on the plants, so divide your goal amount by 100 to get the amount for each.
Each shelf is equal to 25% of the total goal.

Date	Notes	Amount +/-	Balance

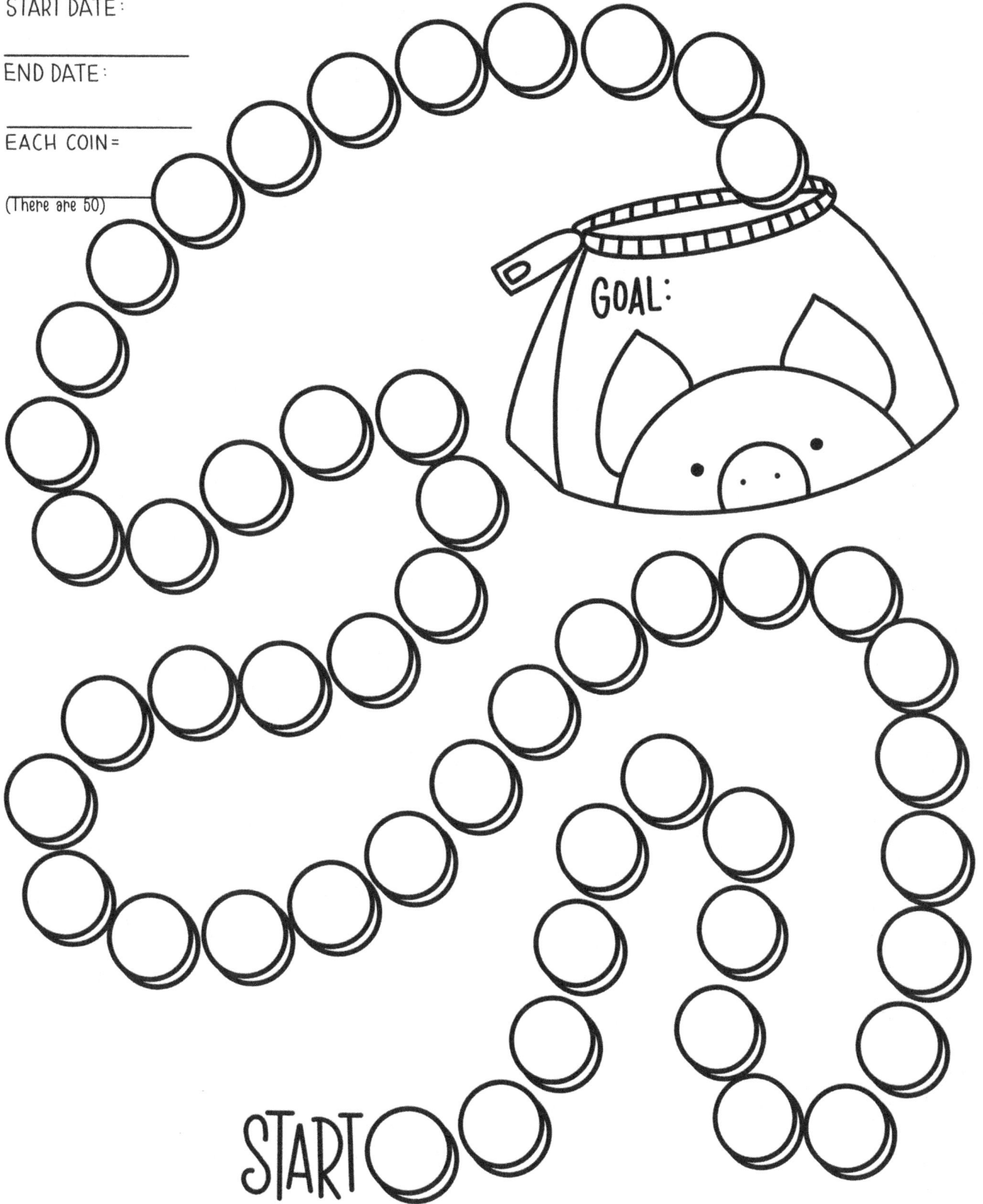

Fill the Piggy Purse
the

START DATE:

_____

END DATE:

_____

EACH COIN=

_____

(There are 50)

GOAL:

START

Fill the Piggy Purse

Savings Goal:	Start Date:	Finish Date:

This game has 50 coins - Use for Savings or Debt
You can divide up your goal by 50 for even amounts, or use it for a 50 Day Challenge, writing in the amount you save/pay off each day.

Date	Notes	Amount +/-	Balance

STACK-MAN

GOAL=

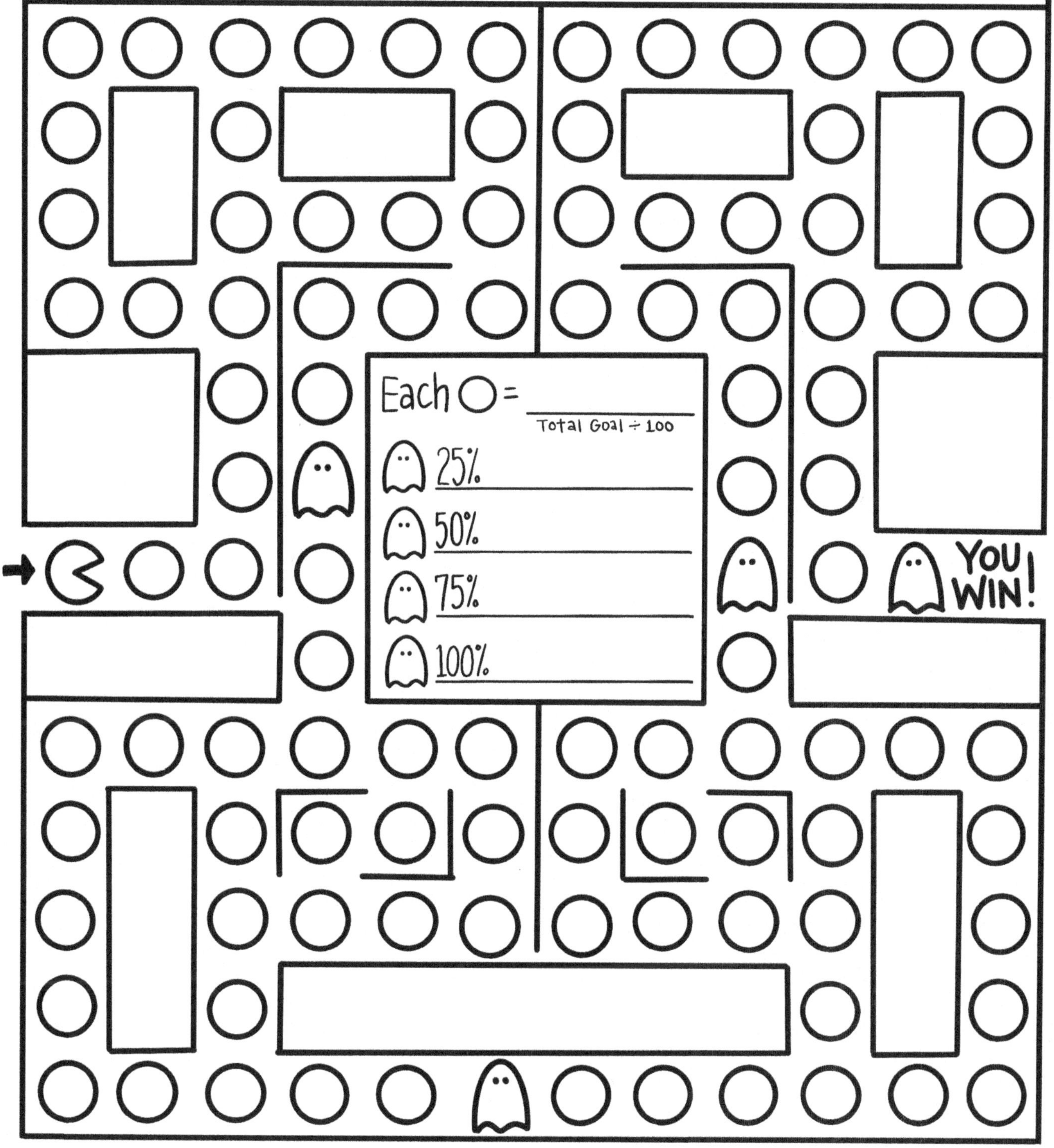
Each ○ =
Total Goal ÷ 100
25%
50%
75%
100%
YOU WIN!

Stack Man

Goal:		Start Date:	Finish Date:

This nostalgic tracker has 100 dots, color in all the dots in a section before you reach a Ghost. The Ghosts are your milestone markers.
Beside the Ghosts you can write in how much is saved when you reach it, or how much is left to save.

Date	Notes	Amount +/-	Balance

30 DAY Savings CHALLENGE

FINISH

START

My Game: _____

My Reward: _____

30 Day Savings Challenge

Here is a quick little planner for you to plan out your Savings Challenge so you have the most success possible.

Decide on what game you are playing -
There are several options to customize your challenges:

- **Even Amounts -** Decide the total for the challenge and divide evenly to get the amount each piece is worth. You can write that amount on each piece if you want. Save that amount daily, or color in several spaces when you save more in a day.

- **Randomized -** Decide on the total for the challenge and divide into random amounts, writing the numbers on the pieces in any order. Color in one space per day, or several adding up to your total daily savings. This is a bit harder to set up, but can be more fun to color in randomly.

- **Save in ascending or descending amounts,** day by day. So day 1 is $1, day 2 is $2, and so on.

- **Save any amount each day,** filling in that day's amount as you go. Add it all up at the end.

Rewards can encourage you to keep going on those hard days. It doesn't have to be expensive, something like going out for coffee or ice cream, or even allowing yourself to spend a guilt-free day reading or binging a mini-series.

Stay accountable by sharing your goals with others -
Accountability is key to success in the 30 Day Savings Challenge. Share your goals with friends or family members who can support you and help keep you accountable. You can also join online communities or forums for support and encouragement.

The 30 Day Savings Challenge is a great way to boost your savings!

My Challenge Game:

Savings Goal

Each Space =

My Reward:

Accountability:

Game Charts Bundle
All 46 Game Style Charts, $43 Value

Big Finance Pack
70+ Pages to Organize it ALL

For dozens of free debt payoff trackers and hundreds of printable charts, trackers, and planners to get your entire money life organized, visit DebtFreeCharts.com

Use the Discount Code MONEYGAMES50 and get 50% off your entire order, even sale items!

Doodle Charts Bundle
All 28 Doodle Style Charts, $56 Value

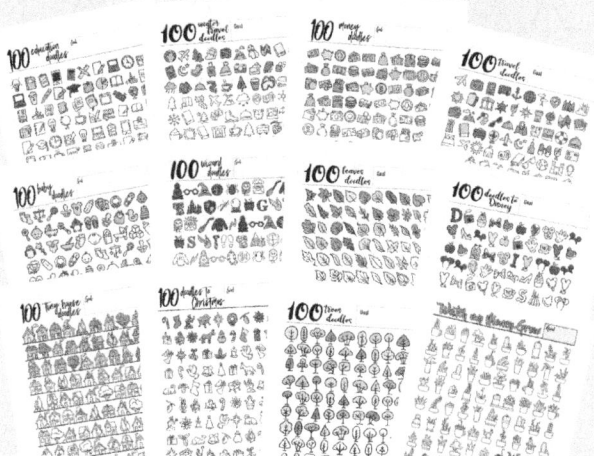

Classic Charts Bundle
All 134 Classic Style Charts, $142 Value

I need your help

I hope this book has inspired and encouraged you, and that it is helping you reach your money goals and have fun doing it. If you'd like to help more people discover this book and try these charts, so they can have fun with their money goals too, please head over to Amazon right now and leave a quick, honest review.

There are millions of people out there struggling with their finances, seeking help, looking for a way to get back on track, and feeling lost and demotivated. You could inspire someone to turn their financial life around.

My mission is to help one million people in achieving their financial goals. And in order to do that, I need to reach them. That's where you come in. By leaving an honest review of this book and the trackers in it, you can help it reach those who need it most.

It won't cost you a single dime and will take less than 60 seconds of your time. But the impact of your review could be massive. Your review could inspire a struggling mom to take the first step towards financial freedom, motivate someone to stay on track to being debt-free, or be the tipping point for a life-changing decision.

So, will you **join me in this mission** to help others achieve their dreams? Will you take a moment right now to leave an honest review of this book and its contents? Your review will help it reach more people and make a real difference in their lives.

To leave your review:
- Go to the Product Page for this book on Amazon.com
- Scroll down to the Reviews section and click the "Write a Customer Review" button
- Write your review
- Add photos or video
- Submit
- When you're done, color in the stars

I can't thank you enough for your support. Your review means the world to me and will make a difference in the lives of countless others. I am your biggest fan and I am forever grateful for your willingness to help spread the word about this life-changing book.

Let's make a difference together!

Heidi

Made in the USA
Monee, IL
28 July 2023